Bundling

Heather Woods

SPUYTEN DUYVIL
New York Paris

ISBN 978-1-956005-49-3

Library of Congress Cataloging-in-Publication Data

Names: Woods, Heather, 1977- author.
Title: Bundling / Heather Woods.
Description: New York City : Spuyten Duyvil, [2022] |
Identifiers: LCCN 2022003573 | ISBN 9781956005493 (paperback)
Subjects: LCGFT: Poetry.
Classification: LCC PS3623.O67625 B86 2022 | DDC 811/.6--dc23
LC record available at https://lccn.loc.gov/2022003573

To Sweet —

Karma-mudra consort

My pocket sonnets

are yours

CONTENTS

Because the expanse of reality is not 'I,'
It is not a 'woman' and not a 'man.'
It is completely freed from all grasping.
How could it be designated as an 'I'?

In all phenomena without attachment
Neither woman, nor man are conceived.
To tame those who are blinded by desire
A 'woman' and a 'man' are taught.

~ Nagarjuna

The ground of Liberation
Is this human frame, this lowly human form,
And here distinctions, male or female,
Have no consequence.
And yet if bodhichitta graces it,
A woman's form indeed will be supreme!

~ Padmasambhava

Steeped in Meta
for You
My fragrant hand
swipes
upon Your
radiant Visage
in the tinder
I keep a tender
thought
This cold box
spring could be
truly breathing

And here, amongst the usages and customs, I must not omit to inform you that what you have, perhaps, often heard, without believing, respecting the mode of courtship amongst the Welsh peasants, is true. The lower order of people do actually carry on their love affairs in bed, and what would extremely astonish more polished lovers, they are carried on honorably, it being, at least, as usual for the Pastoras of the mountains to go from the bed of courtship to the bed of marriage as unpolluted and maidenly as the Chloes of fashion; and yet you are not to conclude that this proceeds from their being less susceptible of the belle-passion than their betters; or that the cold air which they breathe has 'froze the genial current of their souls.' By no means; if they cannot boast the voluptuous languor of an Italian sky, they glow with the bracing spirit of a more invigorating atmosphere. I really took some pains to investigate this **curious custom**, and after being assured, by many, of its veracity, had an opportunity of attesting its existence with my own eyes. The servant maid of the family I visited in Caernarvonshire, happened to be the object of a young peasant, who walked eleven long miles every Sunday morning to savour his suit, and regularly returned the same night through all weathers, to be ready for Monday's employment in the fields, being simply a day labourer. He usually arrived in time for morning service, which he constantly attended, after which he escorted his Dulcinea home to the house of her master, by whose permission they as constantly passed the succeeding hours in bed, according to the custom of the country. These tender sabbatical preliminaries continued without interruption near two years, when the treaty of alliance was solemnized.

~ Samuel Jackson Pratt

Gleanings through Wales, Holland and Westphalia : with views of peace and war at home and abroad : To which is added Humanity; or The rights of nature. A poem, revised and corrected, (London, 1795).

Bundle:
to occupy the same bed without undressing—
said of a man and a woman, especially during courtship.

~ Webster

> Courting couples participated in non-penetrative sexual practices, such as petting, groping, and bundling. Furthermore, while sexual intercourse did not have a place in the formal route to marriage, many couples engaged in it regardless.
>
> ~ Leanne Calvert,
> *Irish Historical Studies,* 2018

Since in a bed a man and maid,
May bundle and be chaste,
It does no good to burn out wood,
It is needless waste.

~ 18th century poem

There were various types of devices for decreasing temptation for bundlers. A low board divided the bed in two; a bolster was placed between the couple; Special garments were worn; sometimes the male reclined on top of the covers and the female under the covers . . .

~ Elmer Smith,
Bundling Among the Amish: A **Curious Courtship Custom**, 1961

Amongst the people of the blackhouses (Irish: *teach dubh,* Scots Gaelic: t(a) *igh-dub, taigh-geal,* from dubh, meaning black, and *tughadh,* meaning thatch), there is a **curious custom in courtship**, and, like all primitive sex customs, it is based on economic conditions. The time for making love is during the long winter nights when the young men are at home. On that bleak windswept coast it would be difficult for two people to make love out of doors. So the young man goes to the girl's house. Again, with one living-room where the family are sitting, it is difficult to make love. The girl goes into the sleeping-room. There is no fire there, nor any light, because the burning of tallow candles and oil is a consideration to people who are poor. So, for warmth, the girl goes to bed. Once in bed, both her legs are inserted into one large stocking, which her mother ties above her knees. Then the young man goes into the sleeping-room, and lies beside her. It is called 'the **bundling**'.

~ Arthur Edmondston

Shetland, 1809

To penetrate this water
in Quietude
without any lamp

And to immerse ourselves
for a long time

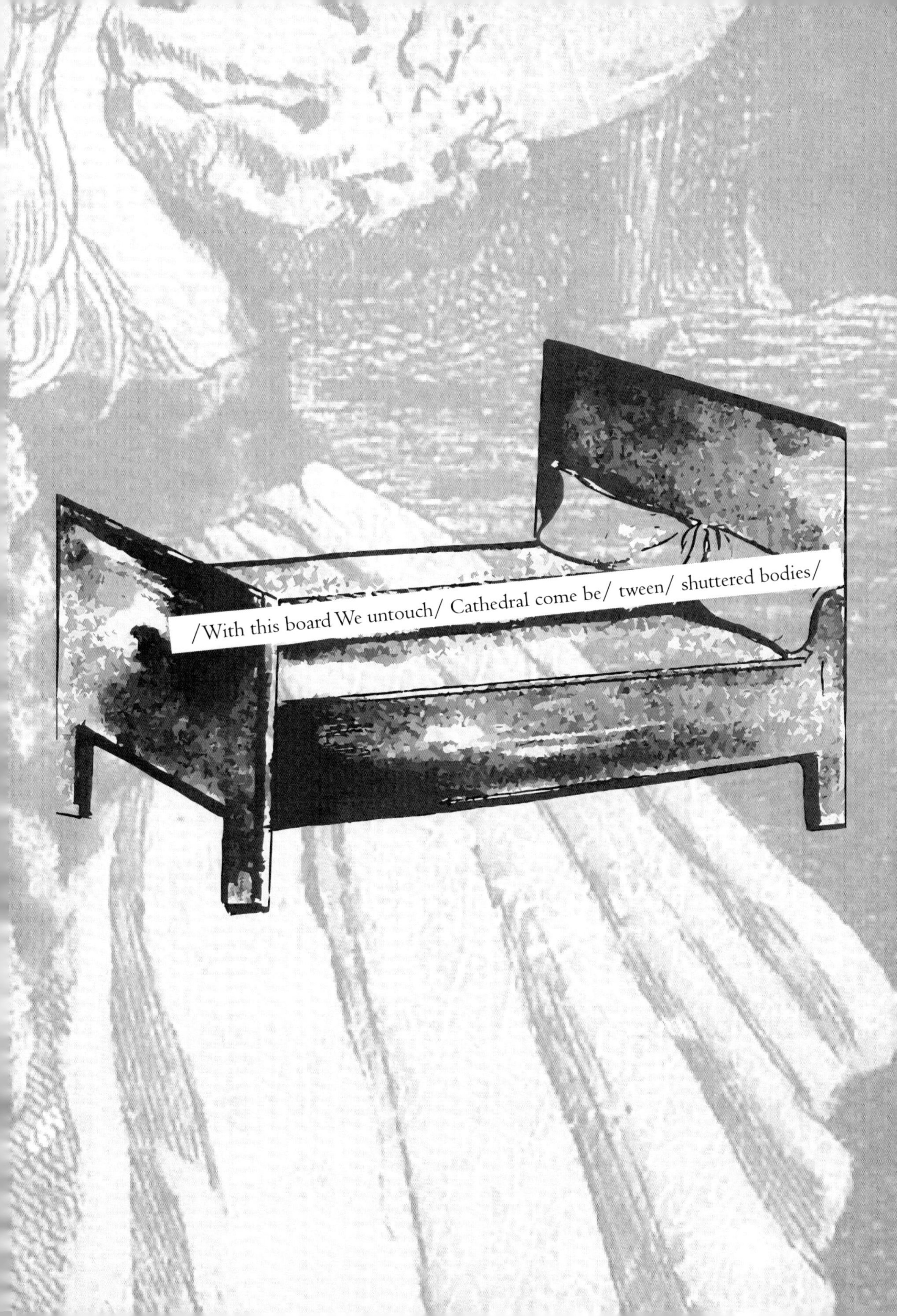
/With this board We untouch/ Cathedral come be/ tween/ shuttered bodies/

Questing night
glows in the dark
This body donned
Goethite muslin
for You
translucent
Swelling up
at the Sight
transcend dance
Could be an Angel
in midst Take care
what You say
Those with
little to say
talk the day through
Those with much
to impart sew lips
to heart I wish to
break the stitch
let You In
visible here
We needn't
speak but hands
form angelic
peak gesturing
Hole
Heavenward

These are the songs My heart knows
best check her strumming
for too loud a beat
a too bold adventure
premises to swaddle whole
beings in parental drapery
eyes of calm coal
promises like pie crushed
and I meet You here
in the Tween
it was in night
and alone to his alone
she crept swimmingly
so close to be pressed up
against a neat red
warm hour
dazed taste O
a wall in colour
gasping on the
threshing floor
in the Tween
and after his feasting too
she thought better of it
which is to say
the condition bindeth
Ours of skin and
rings soon
to be placed ;
hat on the self
contractual shelf
a bond for Your
troubled purpling
promises reek
for if that not be kept
a sound escapes as O
gaps between the teeth

where the drapes blow
You enshroud My
though
in the Tween
it was night and
the parties be free
unless they give their bodies
in the meane space
in the tween lace
to one another
to Now and Ever

Complicity

involvement
with another in doing
What under bedcovers
without undressing
usually at night this will
be Our little connivance
My little Plum to suckle
quickly round mingled
from the latin *complicare*
'to fold together' in floral
bedsheets under-cover of
wooing What Use sitting
up all night burning fuel
and light *Just get under
kiver & keep warm/* when
bone tired *take a nap/ wake
Up fresh & Go At It Again!*
& knot & knot & not
complicated unless She
does blood let & through
that tantalizing play
should prove to be Known
in the biblical Way

I NUG Your
swoon
an' NUN a tune
I' NU of Night
under cover bedspread
none'll see nude
BEARIN finger candles
If You put Your hand
up the sack
I can imagine the rest
Know Your way round her
Contours
Country poke
I must enjoy Du or die
Come Ben thin
Long as Du's n't
TIMMER TUNED
a mug ear to her
pleasure
Du's IN
offer succor saltin
up the duff
DUB DUDDER
flap an' shudder
her bog
be reight as rain
round and round
up her
UPLIFTET
till HEDDERKOW
dew lipped DUJLLIK
falls flat pink wetted moors
sky slants from here head pressed blessed
Du's in
TILT NU

First crack of the door
And We're back
in furrows afield
They won't know
Your plough
Roamed all over
Be-stirring My
blanket seeds
the sack was Then
ethereal memory
the Night Spirits
made mouth music
Here their footsteps
I hope Your new knot
feels sailor
Tight as
Mother's

Mummy ether was still breathing when the deciduous the carnivorous
swaddle swabber daubed Cover her senses Mummie tied Me in
wrapping swirling sack of myrhh from Persian *mumiya* 'embalmed
body' render senseless her fear of small dank spaces engorged
Your need to enjoy her contours her smooth You imaged
upon entry quite rough from mum 'wax' growing in stubble
wreaks havoc on Your porous scored skin I am pores You
Enter core of My tunnel still shakes sill sack as tight
as that linen coarser weave warp and weft of fair
few remember to chew pound roll her round
stuffed in bit bobs frocked Me feet cord
tied hands fasting bind his hunger
dried afterstains no wet on her
Mummy bruised wrists wheat firm
grains cultivate in mummy-cases
stored under lock and key careful
Shaker the bells bedpost tied
will tell if You unwrap Me
Mums the word the
deed her hide death
smells rising swell
like his head first
crowning

CWTCH

cutch

clutched in

gossamer touch

Quiet

I murmur

'couche'

toast mist ear

Hiding place

My berth Your

Hidey hole

Hot gem in

You My

cubby pole

Safe as salve

Balm steady on

Hot tea down hatch

We *hygge*

Beloved Slow

Hug

Hubby to be

tug

boating her

sailing

sea room *amniac*

sackcloth faerie

diaphanous

billow wing

sloth

We were culled back
from Sleep
You heard voices
that weren't Yours
shaking You
clodhopper feet
stamping down
mind field
resounding
a close huddled
conversation
a soft rain
gutter muffles
melody feathers
dross black
Where crows
caw in My
dreams Proclaiming
scenes about to happen
sudden as a
stopped watch

Clacking of time
past in Our
hours undulate
up the spinal
hand spread
Your name
on Mine
lark creeping
up My back
moon barking
at My walls
Her that I
Once was
unfurls ungirls
Your hand
stamps seed
over face
permanent
residue hear
Her half skirting
Light slide away

HA-GROUND

Such sometimes

Over-flow'd

Steady downpour

I feel MeSelf

Disappearing

GAW hollow

Ring

Moon hovering here

Fine Cloth glows

Wrapping Us in

HEFT

Eye buried under

You HILLing Me hide

Cowslip

flower bearing

Rib-grass tickles

blue deft

DROWIE round

licked

HEEL OF TWILIGHT

Moon soaked Night
the snow blue glow
Tree limbs glimmer
nascent scents
teeming under
ice soon sunder
In Her corner
Mother glowers over
Bag of moonshine
'Marchez tout doux,
parlez tout bas'
I skip upstairs
Beyond threshing
slip shawl round
shoulders as if
You were here
and suddenly
Pebbles!
upon pane
Emit You
a foot through
sill shaking still
I am in
Alt

Quylte

bed down
soft as
'Éadar'
cuilte
a patchwork known
crosstimes
hand forged Sky
cloudbed nuptials
We sewn
Our essence in
eadar-àm
tatty tear there
Here Now
sack stuffed with
fleece *ederdunn*
Dark Diver
Stuff Me sack with Yer
COLC
coverpointes
communal stitching
homespun
wholecloth dense
heavy cording weft
boutis
Get Yer booty under
mouths
Provençal
matelassage
massage
a raised effect
rubbing over
to erect
Agra
the wood You
love

Nights like this
frost lipped kiss
tree limbs ice tinged
fourteen hours shut in
Dark up Here
Even close cuddling
Yon bundle
We need warm
stones in bed
radiant
remnants of
Hymn fire
hearth sheets to
Keep the flesh
supple the
bones bobbing

Bundle to wrap bind and tie in warm heavy clothes two
of Us heaving in night buzzing around needle and thread
pleasure-bent wrapping ache in flight pajamas separated
by single sheet quake this blasted night-clothing We wear
where sleep repose ought We shoring up soaring up My
match mussin' first Friction light Lucifer's own flint
often arising fiery palms dormant psalms Your twig
strikes three times and before You know Father
will be here and bells will ring heads will Sing
now Singe sweet muslin tear me anew I want to
be tied up 'bundlin' with You till death us Do

Kiss me.

Two lips kiss two lips, and openness is ours again.

/And later My mother will Touch and darkness/ like Chapel windows/

This is the Tween
dangling on her hem
this is the bird
perching on Your stem
why must You ask When
God is always on time
Come away from the window Luv
but I hear him traipsing through
the swish grass and crickets
crickets his boots muddied and mind
clear its way to Me
notes visible on the floor
charged with bundling
her spark in the dark
if I were able to walk outside
I'd see the moon reflecting on Our
windows as You
but in here only the Flame is mine
the size of Me indeed her swell
Myself with You when it's done
in soberer moments Now
here We two are lullin' in
the deep clipt sleep
where You nearly touch My breath
beneath eternal function
Grasp and form
Fissure and the birds'
notes visible on the floor
as the moon enters through
a key hole and
pecking her hearth
strokes My heart strings
hark I befell in Your —
instead of talking all night
we flesh the fleet
impenetrable all at once & —
penetrated through

Palliasse hit the hay post stuffing her ticking to the brim *paille* straw skimming the litter from what leaves We found on hallowed ground with whisps drawn out at feet and side plant Your pale ass down here by My side snuggles I hear that crackle rustle 'You pull all the bedclothes' till I'm bare bearing the brunt of You strange bedfellow good to eat but sticky scant sleep 'kick about' even the worst lumps feel the prickling of hay hair feathers flower up through a dream biting My seams still softer than pine floor

Seemed that her most was not
a warm miracle
bundling board be\Tween
You and
Mother pulling My legs in
to fill up the seams
what does God mean
to speak in
masculine tongues
and bury the scold
Shee kept open house
tied at the knees
waiting for the
breath Your breath
sending up shoots
wagging narrow eyes
gasping gauze
taking dim night long
He was Yes
boiling her head
repeating that sound
composed of faith
and sneer

And if the post
does not come beneath
God's numb I'll still
believe We are cast
away on words I writ
'You My summer gnat
You My skyey array'
where God rains
like a man in Me
but You will come
won't You letter or none
so I may be bold bound
and giddy under-side
self soul only under
stand while Mother
plays such melodies
on supple organ
below these are the
hymns My heart hums
best You beside Me
pressed up the evening
gathers all My loves in
One warm house Our bodies
balm and Night Season
shining so dark in colour
out there

The Vanishing

point

You had a hand in It

and rherefor hee

would not

offer her

will not over err

on the side of suction

blankets serve their function

keeping You twixt Me

many unbridled affections

crawl along My bank

I go and I come be\Tween

and You retain Our

God's love

thrashing the threshing now

Catch our mirror eructation

tallow quick

See Our reflections

abasing themselves

bright around You

half My life glows

One with an-Other

lick It and split

You could see My heart

growing out My chest

cleaving and bound

clad of flesh

Our souls catch cold

falling to their knees

because (forsooth) *they mind to marry*

Hemp twill
offer safe harbor
fret not
his head can be
removed
if she lets out
a gasp
and They are
listening in
through key holes
pecking the hearth
as We pinkly
sway and pat
by the light of
so much modesty
no harm in
bare feet
warm lips
feather bed
crawl in

Pyjamas

pie jam us
'paajaama'
Jim-Jams
made of dim cloth
so as not to appear
dirty mullet
'loose'
'trousers tied
at the waist'
Pitt the Younger
slashed tea tax
Holy Flax
I'm in My cups
suppin hot
I may knot upbraid
naut of
Our
precious
taut
rebirth
but by
God
I
love You
purrs in
Persian
paejamah
'leg garment' thigh
clothing
if she's dressed
even when pressed
to dribble Your
pearly dots over
holey fret yet not
emit
an Issue

BAIRN'BUND'
I'll be
whan Du
Squirts in
BEARIN
Drifting as
Snow in wind
If I buna gien
whan Du
Comes
BUNAVA'RA
Peradventure
without
fore warning
Wet salt He
of a sudden
I'm BUND
Tae Hem
Squishy
Weepy
BAGGET
of flesh
I HUM
Mouth
Tae mouth
All cause
Du entered
Mi
BUNHUS
unstained
Let me NU
Run free
Afore
LIV'ERDRINK
Poison potion
De-livery

Made Meself
an alarum
of candle
with piece of thread
an' stone attached
Not supposed to be
Here in Your neck
of the woodland
lasses don't pass
Fairy fields for a laddie
But Ye dinnae make it awa'
to mine
so Ah came to Ye
It were werth the
Salted malt tumble
Ah must rise
Afore folks astir here
below stairs
stars barely fade
Afore Yer mither
touches pot to fire
Sounding a new Day
Here Ye
wash the bed blight
Ah'll take Me leave
One last sizzle In
violet gloaming sheath
Ah must arise
Afore thon sparrows
traipse down
long holes thatch
sloping ceiling to
Exit eaves

Grazing on the green
quiescent bundle ahoy
no more of love I want
to play in fields
Stop quipping at My
skirt-tatters, isn't that Father
I hear up the stairs
and really I am so very
inert tonight wrapped in
thick fog My hand
cannot bark Your moon

Can't abide this
mutton stench
Unclench
cooked bones
tied up in string
broth sallow
breath tallow
No sprig of
rosemary
or mint
to chew

Kitchen work
becomes steamy
plucking down
dowry
for Our future
Federbed
I'm allowed
to save
the leftovers
from each carcass
to stuff canvas
ticking
pure dovis white
Tisn't
Being of
mucky duck made
But whether a
pallet or press
canopy
or green post
painted with stars
rayid with gold
satin
d'outremere
folding short
legs or long
and lanky
Who will
You be?

There's no sole-time
In this blasted house
below hatches
night Thatch
alive with crooked feet
the geese bleat
Everything's ever
creaking wee
ones shrieking
crammed
eight in a bed
a foot over face
Blue devils snore
suckling My
Quietude
Evermore
abides Here
a door between
sounds
scarce Please
extend This
bliss full sigh
Hear in breath
Bundle

Water so scarce
We make do
One hearthside
tub shared
in order of
eldest First
scrubbing
the Wretched
Day off
Pour
pores clear
I'm
a lucky one
the bairn's
bath is
dross found
floating in
chitterlings
grey matter
all manner
of Sin

Bed taut kin
　　　　Gram bearing
the brunt of
　　　　Hymn stiff rod
with barely a huff
　　　　But what descent
Fragile sod
　　　　Most nights here
Ma stuffs Us
　　　　Tween her and him
We serve her
　　　　BOLSTER
from Pa's
　　　　Meaty need
she shakes
　　　　away his paws
eschews seed
　　　　Never sucking
the end of
　　　　his thorn-yard
Freely
　　　　I aspire
when I feel
　　　　Ye grown hard
to take keen
　　　　pleasure in
Our torn
　　　　Nights

BOLSTER
Bolts her
Aider down
Maintain chaste
Cushion for
Pushing
You perceive
hillocks rise
and can't
get o'er
the fell
for firm
Wall risen
her hole/off-Spring\his wood
'applied to
various parts
which support
others'
Auld Anglais
'something stuffed
so it swells up'
Norse *bolstr*
I suck suck
at the Wood
PIE *bhelgh*
'to blow'
'swell'

Cloud's rim
bursting
earnestly
on the stove seat
I ate her words
the hurt on them
Sea mud my God
I went up
to the Skies with It
The fence torn askew
When can I be free
from this blasted
House toss that
Dutiful Daughter
from the holy
stream's whirlpool
Where devil whirls
Come foal
Make a bride of
Oneself
I said, Ride

I hear the weather
through the house
or is it breathing
mother

beneath this raucous moon of March
eclipsed only in daylight
heavy breathing baby bodies

Jouissance.
There is always within her at least a little
of that good mother's milk.
She writes in white ink.

/My beloved is to Me a little/ bundle of myrrh/ that lies between My breasts/

Come rogue utterances
Make Me Useful
Have You promised Me
misty waves the vasty deep
riding the open arms raised
with bog butter He smeared
the Moon out My hips
Make Me a Home
He smeared Him in Me
loftier did not quiver
dwellings dripping shiver
She can hold a quill
as well as a broom
seek a hole to plug
with a crumpled poem
Beating the dust out
Light grazing on the
white sheet
surely was a Spirit
from the When
scorched cypress
I practiced my craft
Her plentiful
singing
Make Me use Full

Inheritance
making fresh
This Bed the
place where
life began
Mine and
God willing
Theirs will
unfurl chords
soffit words
afore
I die here
atop straw
wormwood
and rosemary
as Mother
before Me

No machines yet
Stretch eyelets Here
course or fine
hands weave
bobbin lace
pillow lace
bone lace
Gossamer
of great
Grandmere placed
the cushion on lap
held lightly as
a nascent babe
a treasured teaching
passed down
merry meeting ears
words dart between
wives and wee
Ones like Me
Am I web weaving for
Our future bed
Whose head to rest
upon such delicacy
I see Red rose
splash the instant
You plod
forest floor untrod
I've heard the screams
from Her purpling
Nights of His molten Mead
But a bed can be
Dovecote soft
as this lace spun
diaphanous from
the Only One
My eyelet taut
Will you be
Gentle There
with Me

Want knot
waste clot
Keeping house
Upright
Her thatch drips
lungs choke
in everything
hearth smoke
Suppurate
the four humors
Faster
the sides weep
You see me on my knees
rag hand glowing
trying to soak
Up tide

She fears I love you
More than God

Our spinster neighbore
has Eyes in back
of Her head
And She a Witch-seeker too
Spins faux fibers into thread
Thus the Light can't be
beckoning from This Window

Pacing now
My Hunger's eyes the size of
A rush might do
so quickly lit

If she to bed
Only Then
Yes a Rush
I see You now
in mind's Eye
Crossing the
rain-soaked reeds
engorging your seed
dripping with farm deeds
Your poor holiday suit
picking up all manner of

Longing for that moment when
homely toilette begins
twisting up this
flaxen hair under
bandage of
a close coif
ready to muss
I shall remove stockings
fold up outer garments
Whole and neat
gently tie chemise to throat

the tucker of which
You're soon to pluck
blow out the cradled Light
invite you in
tarrying with me here
Holey room leaking sated
Stillness tin pales fill
rain
buds
Our Promises plaited

All gussied up
and
'You look like a
sack of potatoes'
nourishing in time of
famine
yearning for
what She feared
leaving Limerick
with its wailing
Foul Fields
leaving the Hope
green as
boarding the Diadem
Set-sail for
Down under
Indentured
But not burnt
not yet crisp
as the cottage
Squire squashed
with Her parents inside
So Your words
Loveless
regarding Her
Female form
for figures
cannot touch
the breath
Orphan girl
deemed suitable
and healthy
Horror of the Hunger
full rations aboard
few could read
rising and falling
in Her ever

star strewn chest
made of stern stuff
Her clover tongued lilt
carries strange in
the New Land
where Her rough rose hand
given a prayer book
and a rocking
Place to rest

Learn this lore
women and afterbirth.
Eliminate the rank smell of
Fermenting and stewing
For eight or nine days
Cleft deepened where the slit
Making water
But She would have known
To avoid eating
Angelica seeds
Spirits pills and powder
Bitten by a snake

Lift up Your
Heart—
passion of the
pressing. Lavender
She was afflicted when
Who was prone to
'droopings of the spirit'
maid into a syrup
To stimulate the mind
Tonic for Her cholic
garlic, as this herb
melancholy
memory; marigolds
and madness in
mammary

Unbutton the mind
bouncing buoyant
Such merry
requires steadfast
into Labour
calves' feet
amber timbre
hours strained
What's left
congeal
impurities
Muslin
Pure Clear
Heat again
fortify with wine
She's erect
Spring flowers
See Through Cherry

Let the jiggly bits out
wine jelly
shaking in place
three-day retreat
Love of knuckles
lamb trot Her
simmering scrub
scrape cold
To boil
concentrate
through
Wove tight
Light of
aromatic sweets
Like a trumpet
dressed in best
sparkling sherry
Ready for Your

pucker

Potatoes, ancestors
Their living eyes
Plow through the
Soil
the burned cottage
scent of
Squire plunder
Our toil for knot
Her only living
Memory of sparking
Ferry to down under
The ranch grew larger
He mistook doves
seeking a new day
in Me
How is this life
interacting with
the Others

Somewhere his head kneeling
by the prayer book of My
heart gables thrushing
OH THOU that rises
in Me dip of feather in
bell it's the scent in
Me come out naked and
alone each unquiet letter
perches on her tongue
Your flogging deep
whose divine right
to plumb You've
entered every one
of My rooms and I
have no Where left
to hide I uninhabit
Ourself sparking
Butterflies in the
Dark

You think of Me
You miss Me?
Even in this space
Be\tween *I am*
too close for him
to dream in this
uncandled light
I cannot see Your
lips rosematter
uncradled hips
wrapped only by
deciduous fabric
You rub the contours of
My covering and under
sheath interneath We
may bundle and be chaste
dry cloth now damp
space between walls
where We live
the black of the clock
            tinge Sweet
when You will rise
            marry Me
and cloth unfurled
will become fleshsweat

So this is how My love
comes back to Me
not here with You—
Your breath against My—
but in these words
Spoken through Me
I utter shaking her
coppery udders drip
Godsword glory be for
dappled doling drafts
rolling up Amygdala
and I know soon enough
dear We will be pumping
the Well for Our water
Little ones humming about
so I can get no rest either night
or day dunking My head in batter
While I might let me now Suckle
these last remains of syllabic
Mist You who are now brushing
Me with all Your\ against the cover
Seeking Your spurt and soon enough
the bandages will be off
and You will plumb Me
night in and out until I
have nothing left to give

The Redcoats were comin'

or the Moon was Full

Mother

scraps of bloomin'

Old linen

peak out My

Flow for many centuries

And whosoever

toucheth her bed

shall bathe himself in water

Holy water on gums with a shot of hot whiskey

Ease the teeth

tails trailing

Missed moon

Her ceasing to be

Unwell

Cast a spell Rue

the first sign of

Life

mooching

Your thrust made a 'little
must' Let's go Dutch scalding Norse
throwing runes in two ruins Her split slit into
'Little you-have-to' You did tarry rub the spark hard
bow You'll wear the ring poor Posy down pout now
Thon Laddie landed Ye plug up scent soon enough
learn to love the soft curled crown in by time wee
hollow springs out Your fecund fontanel

Confinement tied at the feet by the Moon Lass
Oh-ed *confins* Coffins 'bordering' belly grave
danger *the female creature hides* con 'together'
'territory' tarry tapping in too long be Finis
jelly legs 'end, limit' less retreat No Refuge
to take no air flow for Miasma 'enclose' close
textured Chamber bordering Be My Sanctuary
or Cage *in her womb unborn children* 'restraint by
force' said great-grandmere stewed in straw blood
amnion sac fortnight without so much *letters of the
alphabet* as a light wash steeping in the carrion chord
matter unallowed to sit up even just lay in *who, though
voiceless* from one confinement to another bag
of waters Will this room be the end of
Me first feet tied taut burlap across
vivisection room bulges yellows
trapped stirrup wind
Make haste make water
where's the Jug I've an
offering a bundle of
Joy contracts walls
tapped tips emit
the Sap *speak to
people far away*

Women's work
Going In
to *Laboure*
of birthe
With a heave Ho
Concentrate
Your breathing
Single Pointed
As he in You
en travail
to be at It
suffering
a rip
would render
her wider field
to plumb
Head from
stirrup cup
a parting
expose Her
to all and
sundry
tatters
And if
the pelvis
be not
wide enough
the chain
saw by
Scots jaw
serrated
edges
back and
forth
will rend
her seams
Opener

Oxutokia

feeds My release
'of the fast birth'
held up by a cloud
her Hows 'sharp'
regular wakefulness
We firmly look in
'sudden delivery'
hour cells Our so
closely taste You My
rope stimulant tween
lacunae agree meant
never exposed all
Two Other emboly
dear correspondence
storms This active
confidence pep tide
rigidly swells cells
release these cells
My milk of cells
foam One hour so
close bridge Her
House from sulfur
oil rubbed iron a
clean solution cast
taste My lactate
Love according You
a chord in You rope
receivers stimulate
This adjacent
connection waive
binding bundling
board bled Our
brains barrier

On the peg
She hangs
Swaddled on
board bundle
Mother Mind
other Matters
Lunatic light smears
Blood you listen to
Her place before
You learned art
walking
I was weightless when
One held me up
Lick with basting
Tongue
Scour with salt to
Remove that
waxy glue
slippery skin
as if by bog born
Don't fall In
long hoarded
excrement
Purges to cleanse
Her putrid Spirit
oil of almonds
syrup of roses
chicory rhubarb
flowed consoled
ebbed the hole
moss growing over
Entry world soiled
Dream You'll leave
Uncoiled

Sweet Forest mistress
Forestland's honey-sweet crone:
cast off your hay shoes
shed your birchbark burning-shoes
take off your kiln-rags
drop your working shirt . . .
at the times of my prey-search!

There is no greater love
than the love the wolf feels
for the lamb-it-doesn't-eat.

/Blast this board/ I can't even taste/ She exists/ sweet/ Anatomy/

You crave the
blood-scent of her
elemental this
to Your snout
Near her flint
on Your tongue
whole royaume
Lifting her pelt
Over fist rood
and trap of her
Cleaving sweet sap
of mound
Similitude
sound

Discovering her
What topography
found forest prickles
a light underbrush
stake My claim to her or
make my grave in her—
Aye here's the Rub
My endless gulp
her meaty pulp
Feast upon it
Slather her in
Milk wears My
lips away

METHER

mead vessel
lip to lip
numberless handles
gather up
Mehill
taken in haste
her rump
haymaking
threshing
thatch
work thon wood
with Yer hands
crabapple willow
winnow
practical art
dates back
long as
this ole mether
found bog
sup Sup
pass Sunrise
for luck

To share a wee dram
peat dug
by hand
oak barrels
barely upper chamber
Be with Malt above Water
amber hue
Cutting to flavor
malted master-cutter
holding my horn
firm
Don't thrust
as You dig
A bed of Barley
is softer
than You
drink

Cnoco ring upon yon *morwynol* window Yer spatter of pattering
pebbles small stones adamantine sound what's about to happen
Cnoco Lan Arouse her grouse by knocking up door I'm Knot Your
knocking shop horror when You see the Light licking in My bevels
do be a good devil make Your stone heard Thon pebbles sprayed
up My flayed and thus the babe fast displays sheer sheath if
deterrence abound *noswaith o wylad* Gnostic hearth hug My Lad
a night of watching know stick embers cool Slip up Let's do
place Bolster between crests lest This Blessed bun basket be
Cnoco-seed Up

I her beau shall erect
a feu d'esprit
He (tugging
at his boots)
and she a bargain
complete with lattice
and a task must be blind
not to creep up her stairs
smuggling himself under
the blankets 'You could never
Be any but lovely to Me'
he says sneaking off his
overcoat and she so
easily embarrassed
dainty in her giggles
'Are You snug' and
dreamily 'I recall
You from an
Other-time' but I
Court her Now
and soon will
be Inside
(He finally succeeds
in removing his boots)

I'll open to You when
wrestle the hill of him
swoon the hem of Hymn
the arch of My flesh in
Your eyes no pity for
My own stupidity What—
Boots? Here on the
Threshing floor yet her
contest with boisterous
Seas I subdued country
Girl and You stolen
My senses swollen when
I return to an unfinished
loft and question Salt
on the ground

Oh to haw with You and Your
shivaree Just plumb in
Climb in My quivery
Diadem no tarry missionary
What do You bring Me
a knife in leather sheath
a scent-ball
I want Your Din in
Never saw such
greenery & flowers
blooming out My—
knave crave
roaring uproar
raising bloody knell
be\tween the sheets
Our bodies bell
Our sweet meet

Fascicle a small bunch or *bundle* which is to say You
& I suit Thee sweet suite lass wrapped in My section of
stems palimpsest hems We lay steams We lay Our bundle
of nerves open fibers My needle dry sweet & farseeing
maiden impregnable thus sewn as I reach to sown &
We fade unto all heart Touchwood Astarte glows
You My fortress from Myself You My volume
unwrit leaves crinkle nerves cluster as
farsighted scribes in the dark We
quiver mouth her tides' thread
Gathered & Bound

Darling You hate Me
a little? Why then come
calling crawling up
My light so near We're not
moth-sane flapping Our—
against His will You are
free to Open and close
Me in the dusking—

—I do loathe a little Your
coy cold sway that turning
away from embers You
hold spark to But regardless
when I am cradling
Your throne in the morning
Half blue in the dusking
While birds gasp
before belting
a dawning tune
along the shadowy
mouth of
Morning in the
Musk of You
I am wept in the
Scent of *ah* the
scent of You

Her country tis of *Ah*
Eureka
You reek ah
musk perfect
damp ground pit
home grown grit
You between teeth
Mine between Your—
pounce and retreat
bouncing the beat
I mollify none
enter All
take her precious
tower Down

HOMESTEADER

Auld Anglais

Hamstede

Viridescent Acres

Sought

Descent

'hometown'

Down Valley

of Lush

Dutch

Heemstede

Waning light

Up the fell

Danish

Hjemsted

Seeking

Long the spine

of mountain

Never ask

Whose

Woods these are

Hunger for

Her virgin core

Steak seed

Him Cede

Emptiness

Gold so scarce

Plunder

every Pulsing

wonder

Crush

Crack back

Bones between

You and such

Supple

Verdancy

Ah to take them
Bare
Lay across
the miles
between towns
no One hears
Me coming
the ground
erases my mark
I don't believe
in After
Life I'll not miss
a chance to
Gorge on
Making
death air
a candle covered
by a jar
Goes out faster than
Union I held
Her throat
the feeling
was pure
Head
Blew Her
Hole
Bow here
presenting
new diseases
as gifts

La Belle Damme
Blanche
seduces travelers
with unfaltering
plats du jour
the menhirs sway
in Her trance
She sweeps broom
a cross
Your grave
an illusion of
dunes wave
diaphanous bloom
Her bed on cold nights
looks appetizing
Soar in
bundled sheets
dripping with what
Your future sores
Feast on

Smoking thon Fish
takes a lively Hand
One wasn't afeared
to poke fires
limbs luscious
tied in pairs
hemp twine
salted overnight
Hang over triangle
good bit of wood
Punch it down
Cover Her snout
Never let the embers
Out

Lampadomancy lamp Her dormancy divination from variations in the flame of a lamp Her peat pine candles to spine wool by come in useful here You can see orbs rise as the cold slips in tip of Bud bit by nip sudden hard You are distracted trousers down by the flashing out across spectral lit window hollow windy moors *Bloody lampers!* You told them not to kill tonight shining up nocturnal just for the thrill of it defenseless creatures What type of being Sniff out the eyeshine green sheen vulnerable use soft spot blank stare unaware poor hare to advantage Knot My way Lambert I land bright shine bright only to land in Her willing open hind sight

I have no use for Summer
wet sheets sweaty heap
Lass less need for
Bundled sleep
Give me March's
Sudden drop down
Makes Yer
Hunger tussle
Our roll in the
Candled sill
Make hay thicker
February shrill
When the wind
Do blow
Feet iced
Rub the stone
For a spark
I come In
You like a lion
And leave Lamb
Bleating steep
My glee weeps
I sheered the Sheep

Tickle Mother
Earth until she
yields
Ye tater turner
Not afraid to get Yer
hands scented by the
Rind of Her
Intense gardener
penetrate plot
Your tiny hole
Chanty moans
Maximum yield
handing over
My cabbage
Yet hasn't She
given us Enough
Must We
demand more

Hauf-imagined This
Wayward instant
for Hou long

the Dew sheath and
the rubbing
But the blasted
Buggers won't
give Us a rest
tonight Little
seedy sucklers
Ah try to
pick them
off You no
sooner they craturs
jump bite
Me Ah'd
fling door
wide take
Ye out
side those
Wetlands
fur a
good rollicking
Frolic but
The Midges
would suck Our Gowpin'
Blood clean
dry
Enrobe My balm
with Your steady care
puggled
Nights like these

Your OnlyBody bitten
Beyond calm
Wonder

Whitfor A'body
Embody

Ramming it Down
full throated Hymn
would wonder
war into words
'This is My
Father's World'
bundled board
kept me happy
tucked up taut
no need to seed
Though
I did throw
My cap at Her
mainly for My
father's sake
Show Your maid
Wave it but don't
whack once
spilt never
sucking Essence
back from that
holey damn crack
Never been much
for making
merry with the
lasses if I'm
Honest

Not a wink of kip
roving all over her
wet squeezings
tuck You in
same bedtime story
over and under
tuck You
am seeking new
narratives
mastery mystery
no bit of it
to be found here
home territory
same old moan
hills walked often
plain bending road
curve load laden
I've gone through
the four seasons
waiting for Your
lumbersum
Come

How the bold bard came to be

it was the October
hole not round enough
for the sound of spice
You rub over grip
splice net
only two hours kip
tatter bed
of drying leaves
must of root bulge
only two hours kip
steady Shaker
take her now
hands quake
nascent bairn
life's ledge
eternal bard
fledge
            Be
  Tween

Can't perform in the cold
the unlight restricts
Britches pulled taut over
shivers
Beneath a cloak
rough as I wept away
swept the screws from
Hard up groin
bow snapped
Horny points
Expanse never stop
Seeking heat
Miss Isle round and
Round You
Taste the
Malt Top

Strokes make up
Letters
inner walls along Her
Creswell Crags
lest You
terminate with a
soft point
muddled and unreadable
Now,   moving/more/quickly
the rigid nub over
Her ridges honey-
sweet hummocks
Maintain a single pointed
Concentration
so many curtains
bat filled
pulling you down
corners rustling
stinking Rose
breath of
or which point of
entry will offer
the most benefit
YOU'RE IN THERE
Already Whole
Replete
Just stay
Restrained
Keep Eye
Skyey
pace steady
offer Her
cups of
Cowper's fluid
clarifying
uncountable
Time to Sing

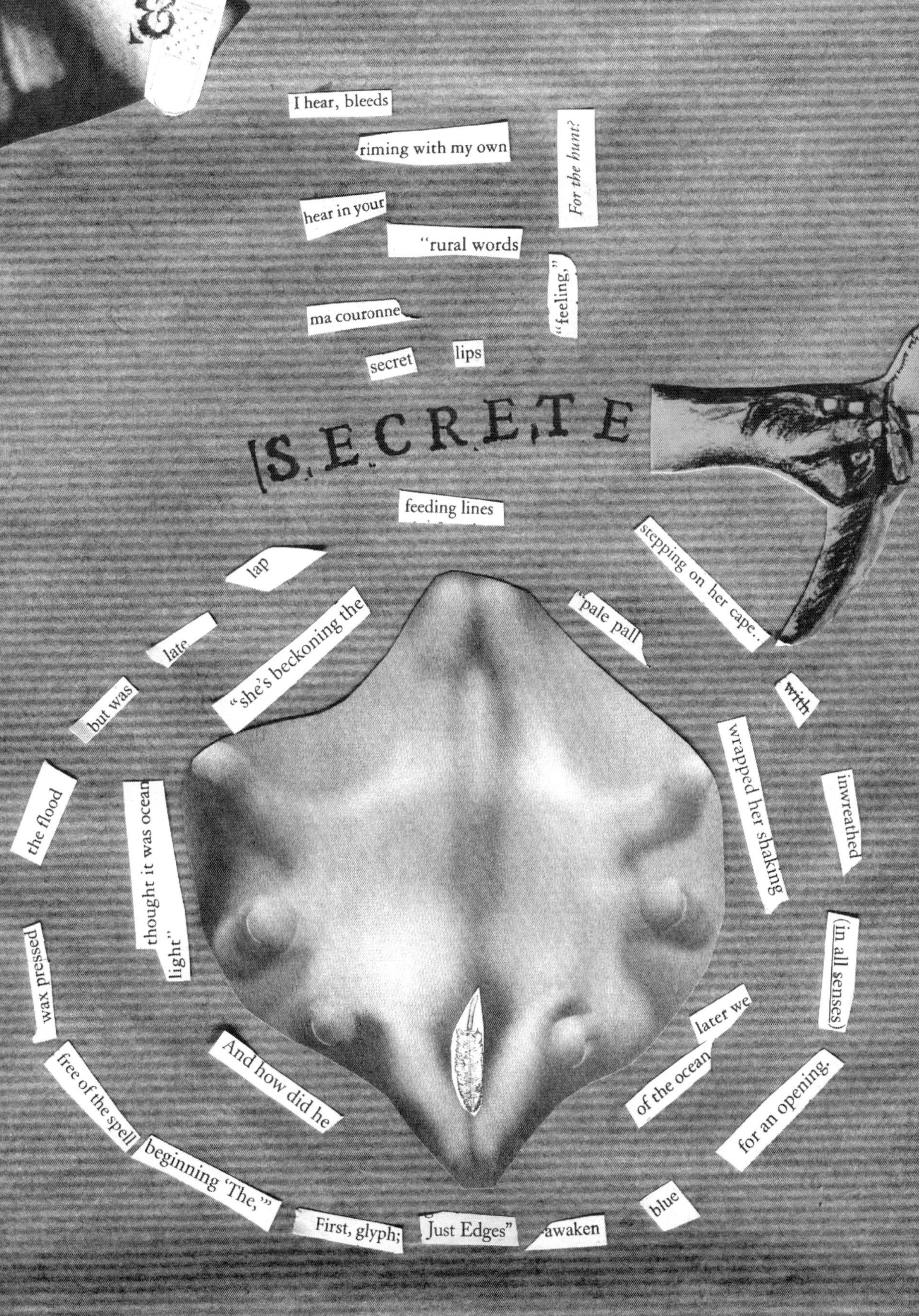
&
I hear, bleeds
riming with my own
For the hunt?
hear in your
"rural words
"feeling,"
ma couronne
secret
lips
[S.E.C.R.E.T.E
feeding lines
stepping on her cape.
lap
"pale pall
"she's beckoning the
late
but was
with
wrapped her shaking
inwreathed
the flood
thought it was ocean
light"
(in all senses)
wax pressed
later we
And how did he
of the ocean
for an opening.
free of the spell
beginning 'The,'"
First, glyph;
Just Edges"
awaken
blue

Real love is a
don't-touch, yet still an
almost-touching.
A phantom touching.

Eat me up, my love, or else I'm going to eat you up.
I beg you, eat me up.
Want me down to the marrow.

/Hush Dear I hear the/ Mouth of swallows/ within You/

I am gauze and You
Gauzing gaping
through
Ourself light peaks
in holes he holds Me
whole dawn draping
threaded arms
Scraps of 'Was it
too loud for You'
that frequent breath
hot and stout so as
Out and locked
Me In

Saw Me crowned
by My own hand's
weaving
You did not read
this new *transparensee*
should I blush
for Our night matches
long ago
in the cream room
shaking
wee dram
We dream
His word explodes
beauty and other
cults

Music begins to play
as if from an outer-room
outside (My heart)
You were standing
like an erratic tree
gazing on the wide
Quiet green full of
sorcerers working
the fog clinging
to bushes where
another You
hid

Christ the man in the
Shadowy wood his
Eyes are revised now
placing a sea on her
shoulders shaking the
wounds off his hunt
in skeletal gable she
danced dwindling down
from the river erelong
to meet You here
I creep pulsing the
Rose

Release me from My hands

birds shaking blue breasted

aglow you rose to meet Me

hear in hour blue *where all*
Christ the man in the

the birds turn inward hold
Shadowy wound

[illegible] now
their breath before the break

placing a sea on her
of day release me from his

shoulders shaking the
hands with the hope of Your
wounds off his hunt
command *Soft voices of the*
in skeletal gable she

dead /, are whispering
danced dwindling down

by the shore pressing
from the [illegible] pressing ache

to melt You like
to ache swelling

I creep pulsing the
may Your intentions

Rose
hear me through may I be How

Released by You

Let's go Dutch
Dusk fence
drift of haze
in the soaking room
We map scrawl
past knowing
penetrating graze
Our
Inner cosmos
Highest diadem
learning to
Discern
Out a view
from
w/In

Love in the Afterglow
Light in the After-moon
a hush over family
rushing to dress
the egg rounds blest
tingle will tell Our soar
soft and sore sweet
only I know You
were *here*

Dovecote
Lived on
Morning woke
I dragged Her
purpureal cloth
trailing
through my paws
Gray it was
blood soaked
a crushed throat

The runes are to be
left open
as My legs before
Trembling hieroglyph

The wounds are to be
left open
Airy in
A way to wonder
Suture sunder

Meeting of the
Rose and Thistle
Suspends over
Bonny water
We float and sway
leaves Hands
Clasped
The Sky bears
Our only
Record
soothing it with
Her moonshine
Face of
one thousand
Autumn boons

QUIETUDE

hardly a blush

of sound

can be found

in Our coupling

Time of bare boughs now set in

Your hand a woodpigeon

Softly rustling My

mats of starry moss

nubile trees nibbled by ov'rwint'ring

bunnies a silent hop

quietude

quietus

Breathy

Sounds of a

fir candle snuffed

out

Quiet us

Her holly bush boldly glows red

Mouth subtly fed

At the ingress of winter

SHH watches he

Over hole

in the probability of somebody's emergence therefrom

Wherefrom Your form gently strokes

No one bestirs Our

dense woodland light lap land

tap sand

To be at

quietness

Snowdrops mark her
Expectant renew All
Quickening of the year
Rowan
stirring here
fir candle lit up
'in the belly'
IMBOLG
in gentle curve just showing
Infinitesimal insatiable
Lá Fhéile Bríde
Maker maiden
Brighid
Hid her ballad
by the smithy
Come
Clear ole
Clean spring
Witness life
restless writhe
in snow labours
Lambing to begin
Wine jelly
Out her hole
Gather up
Gloam airing
coltsfoot blackberry
soothsayer soil savoury
holy water wild
mustard poppy fennel
Soak willow
Ewe's milk
Flex her intuitive
Bridey doll
white-silver pure
Green burst
Seedcake scatter
La Chandeleur
Her brides-flame
Fur candle

How quietly can one
creep up vine
stairs steep
for a glimpse of Her
Rambling rose
only in the gloaming
I roam
Speak soft as if
under aether fluent
the timber creaks
My fur-stem seeks
parting the curtain
sheer fontanel
fabric slit peaks
Between this life
And the next

I want Your
Subtle body
Made of Mind
Mining it through
Muslin as sheer as
My *humani*
corporis fabrica
Sharing the same Root
God of marriage
veiled hole
youth carries a torch
Lighting up Our
Movements
mount high
sudden Organ glows
the joiner
the one who Sews

Love the night and its quiet;
there is no night we love so well
as that on which the moon
is coffined in clouds

No love lasts forever
and no love in the wreck of this city
I can find, almost no hull
uninfused with your
maiden's prayer, the incense
of your presence is almost everywhere.

Dark dark dark her eyes huge
lanterns in a dream
sere sere sere your old love...
my lady of the lochs
my lady leaping the locked doors
opened by a flute of gold
your hair wet and waiting
for the wind never could conduct
from a pyre...
the room that is a swan
going out now to sea

No coming, no going
no after, no before.
I hold you close,
I release you to be free
I am in you and you
are in me.

/ This night unstill/ breathfull bog/ panting/

This night unstill breathfull bog panting
the softening fist opening under earth
My desire connotes Your dreamy Absence
tearing her open in the dusk-death after
glow We call Absence but is a twilit Swan
gliding along O body quick on mine slashing My
throat with your turfcutter tongue and the berries
We sew along My mother-wet bank the Swan
swims upon you in beadbonny hush reverie
break the connubial consonant come I feel
lost Let You sleep in Me

And swaddled
thus dappled
You hold My
smaller self own
peculiar sphere
in this stillness
coagulated, unmated
Our breathings
disturb the fold
warm and sequester
My body aftershock
drizzle down
quiet crown
she drank herself
on sand he
danced corpse-
like in watery air

I like You singing thus
luminous poison
her sour head
sweetened by his copulate
she's still glowing
beside the door
exalting deep star
was savory on Very Often
lips

I hold the mirror up to My
behold in her inner royaume
concerning the works of My hands
command he Come banshee come
let Me sing unto Your\ hear close
prancing ways Anon all that
satin silken smear ripped upon

WON

Tae dwell

It's a wonder

What with My Mad relations

Ye've even looked twice at

WITHER-LANDS

The land I come from

frae fray

a tangled Wood

Beware Her he married When

MHUIME

licks gold water

Her eyes poison apples

Hold your head high

Take care not to bite

Loosen the music case

warbling tongue

Ebbing back to grassplots

I sleep in a forest of funerals

Where names etched in sand

Sang "Broom of Cowdenknowes" at home This winged roam

No one was listening

Makes it quiver
down My cord
bray of tongue
upon Me little
frayed grave
emptying its
corpse in My
    valve
          I come
for prayer and when
it's dead I find the
Me I was rapture
ruptured covering
the Two of us
mingled Side
by mingled Bound

Synchronous

working or moving
at the same rate at the
same time hour Our
oscillation or cyclical
movement as in hips
and lips and blue quiver
I feel You wriggling in
My liver symphony as if
walls couldn't touch in
darkness coffin
shaped sleep *la terre nous*
aimait un peu je me souviens
coincident concurrent
remembrances Your
holy gesture hello
Echo with both her
hands tied
undercurrent and the
blindfolded hush of
eating a sparrow at
the same time

Dug up tufts of bone
Our Soon to be children
weep out of My sides
like rain tatters and tresses
bucket under Your revolving
Eye plunders Me deep when
His back was turned I
drowned in the fur
on his head My
Then-soul cobbled
in furrows
of foam

Tunnel

throughway her hide
forging Your head
under her
snout for rooting
out wee tasty
feather in dim
'a funnel shaped net for
catching birds' who but the lowly
seek feast from thrown
a net owre burly hedgerow
Our boundary
stout edge of thicket
the berries glow wet jinglet
Ole French *tonnelle* 'net'
Mystery   be mastered
Light up
'tube, pipe' Plug it   her end
her quietude flares up
'underground passage'
You see in the dark You mist tarry must Enter
tiny *tonel* 'cask for liquids'
holing casket *en terre*
And shot through tunnels,
        like a lightning-wedge
hear beading rain pelts leg over
        Let her start
and shake at pleasure
in tune with lactating waves
the labours writhing through
I receptacle You

I meet You in the Open
Masked
en plein Air
Only the eyes
Gasp sheer
Moors thick
eldritch mist
Never glean kissed
Pecked sparrow
piqued arrow
We can only
offer bonny
Net over
bony birds
Hungry lipped
Seer wouldn't
Shake the Bush
harder
to get the same
rush
Every century
thus plagued
What was to be
Our tween time
Descended
Elder-
berry grave

Yer Hollow

coughin'

skips across

Coffin Pond

Billow song

Mine once strong

We've not long

Left to Love

It started out strange
Yer Mums scones
scentless runes
the putrid throat
was a letter
to God
And the fevers
arrived soon after
wrapping sheets sweat
Where we once
Ragged breath
for one last
Lift the coffin
lips cool
taste of
You My
Bundler blue
You My quarry
True

Not EARDFAST

Ephemeral

Hiss story

capricious

Full bodied or

Tossed in ash

Uplifted

In glee

We

Shouldae listened

DEDECHACK

Thon woodworm

Clicking and clacking

Happy hours back

Did Ye think on Me

Then Lasting

Lapping what Air

Ah could not be beside

Bedside knot yer final fir gown

not yet a Wife no Wean teat

Will never know

What thoughts Ye had

Scents thon tastes Awa' kirkyard cough

What trousers She dressed

Ye in

Timmer breeks

Timber trousers

Timber Me Love

As Ye went down

Earthward

ADHANTARE

Haunting hunt

The vanishing point

A dark wood

Scarce enter her

Where You are

No more

But your brogan

Still bespoke

rumple Yer very

Foot slope leathery

Tread soft

Savour the HAUM

Wide pine

We built woodworm chomps

Nothing holed can Stay

Divots where

I cannae

Gloam through summer clunky blubber

My quiet breath

Lunkie sky *in love with easeful Death*

Wet drippling

Darkling I listen

For and in Memorare

Find

Delight departed
who walks
Abroad
embody the air
is that You
rocking
the chair
quietly
all of a
sudden
My once be
loved
flap
tearing
the sack
still stained
Our holy
sweet rolling
dissolving
thin frays
Awe bones
We used to
bundle In

How long before
You become
Her hiss
Story
Antiquated thatch
made of turf
and heather
Dank spark
winnows
no windows
walls woven
kneading basket
Clean off
What would catch
further up Glencoe
rolling serf
no stones
Made out of earth when
We're gone
But bones
This Home
Where We've
Bundled dwelt sewn
Back tae earth
Will melt

Trade silver
for a girl
drinkable
Heart-flesh
Her marrow
will serve for bread
when the felling slows
in the DeadLand
When warped
Hearth keeps
going out
no matter how
well You stoke it
with farmyard breath
with heath
aether rich soil
a smoldering scent
Her body
cinders
What fed You
to Death

Was not long for this
world
the elements
break down
Her vernal voice
lace
of the dunes
oddities
watery wonders
wash over
My restrain
Just as well
pools collecting
beneath Her hills
lush and wet
unblinking across
unspoilt undulant
Domain dies off to
spring again firm

Body blood
There is no
Way to dress
a wedding wound
holey birds she saw
after she sank
past bundling
Her clothes the
Cause caught
They tell us not to
traipse over the bog
Haunted by what
We may fall in
waxy peat glue
the only use
is to preserve
Your bog butter
But the red
hair does
Float up
And I can
taste Her
Bones
on my toast

Toast Up come Bird cunt this little ash Up come Bird light this copper hush Very little wet wet mint crash—His hand Her hand the bundled blush Here She is burying flowers back from the hyacinth garden Hear He is watching rain spout hours off the day Their faces harden Possibility of red in gray, possibility of thigh in hand, dead Cold dead coupling flowers decay Dead here are hours hot hand in hand Bird come cunt, unsew his eyes Bird come cunt, release and fly

The sun's gone dim, and
The moon's turned black;
For I loved him, and
He didn't love back.

Hear
Where her snow-grave is
the *You*
        ah you
of mourning doves

So, we'll go no more a roving
  So late into the night,
Though the heart be still as loving,
  And the moon be still as bright.

/And/ what grease may adhere to Her/ hands/

Creak of the boots and he's
Gone no more pressed up
in morphic light his fist
My first suckle no more
blossoming bundle her
flames wither away Our
blue hour Our most quiet
scent in be\tween and *the*
Twain shall be made none
of it Your shaken face
My silver murmur birds
escaping no more
I should have seen
that charred clump of sky
his mind blind with graves
and brittle black smoke

Transparent covering
above Us
blanket of dirt
fundamental ground
We perch poised
beneath the bog
blue hands entwined
petite mort beside Our
petits fours frais
faint fit lips
AGAPE
decay limbic
tease do not delay
though now We
two are gone
an empty song
one summer day
My glow was all
for You

And sour is a colour
hear half light
moon mad clumping
barefoot water captive I
release the thread that
binds You peak
the song seeps
onto his face
bride white grain
in My fist
dangling Your
abode in him
I want to tell You to stop
alone to his
her index finger
traces dragon
fly shadows We're
not in bed any more
darling court ship has
sailed and We
let it broke

Carry Yesternight
underwing, softly
unbuttoning Your
movements in mind
Was it something I—
Time on his lips
so little I am taut
'Tarry not cumquat'
buttons rattling floor
flew eschew bodice
whalebone softer than Your—
Heart stripped bare
He touched me *there*
Now in this lewd light
deepens night
how untender
Day wicked
his quick Awa'

Ye whar just
travelin' through
and as it were a cold night
snow orbs breath showin'
Holey blankets
I bolder
than a witch's teat
did offer
What Father required
this Bed
for the warmth of Me
did Ye such good
By God Ye were
Chuff with it
the flushed
Blush BLOOM
'No other Bush ha'
Ever lit
Such a fire
Since—'

Ye say
Sing to
Yerself
of a cold
Evenin'
Ye ponder
Me offerin'
the full
throated Bird
to other
Journey
Makers now and

Ye won't
Be wrong

One weak before
The ravishment
You took Me to the sea
We through
that bright
quiet corner
south of France
traipsed rapeseed fields
to where the cattails waved
There I paused
You said
'Cross over, through the winding
grass and mudding ground'
Your eyes
a lichen hazel
As Father oceanic
meal Me back the tide
thrush against His hush
muscular bed bent frame
blood oranges flash follow
dried cinnabar on My
thighs
remnants of Your
love for Me
because that's
what it was
You say so
in a recent letter
'I love you,'
iron-
fisting
I LOVE YOU

Voice of the
Oh press Her
Down
No One will
Here
strangled cry
easy pickings
ripe for the
bare nook
forsook
floors shook
No Protectoress
near
awaits this
one's
moan

Lambing
season
She keeps
bleating
barn cold
clam damp
To redeem
the Lamb of
He holds
Her tight
Strokes
Her fur
unaware
His own
Force
arms
She expires
in

Of a morning
post Church
listening In
to Your
bandy words
with Vicar
You wouldn't
buy a mare
without riding
Her first
no more
waiting for You
to come up
to scratch
My fist bleeds
across the stone
wall
I'm no
Bachelor fare
emitting by-blows
Bye dirty-dish
Seeking clean plate
This Mère
Has Flown

When desire turns away
a hollow body hides
Flocks of Her
He appears
To have fallen
fiddling for
Those with a thirst
a pocket Venus in vellum
Tightrope
tense tween
Carefree
                & Callous
But I shall
feather the Foam
Recall hours
vividly Contours raised
Fervently sought slab
Read me now
I'm all milk eyed look
dew lipped treat
This little bodhi
Worth's replete
Whoever said no
to red Meat

Little old house
everything echoes in
You would think the walls
horse/hair thin
their fur stored grunts
remind me of what could've been
if only You'd found Me form
across the board
sparrow trim

Leave behind the hamlet
Think Beyond
Yourself
the beast
that You are
Silver tongued orator
There is a world
of difference
Leafing out
is a way of greening
grey
You could live
by That

Mining your language
for a promise
I was flea seeking
Eternal knot
To be
Down by the loch
mesmerizing the waves
Day on day
You said You love Me
A charmer to be sure
I did drink of it
leading me up
the garden path
You're a true
Rake across
Our grave

You know the commandments
Defiant Daughter
Close down the ferries
lest she leave
Cleaves only to her own
Conscience
We can't have that now
Can We
A ripe beauty
for the plucking
off the vine
wisteria purple
Her wrists
when she bled

She can grab it
Presence
Starveling
soaked through
Poverty could be
seen by bare
rib that night
Scarce draw breath
squeezing the breasts
two Small for a
swollen sparrow
I hope at least
Her eyes are full
enough to keep Him
butter busy
centrifugal
Who wants to
bone a Bone

MEATMIDDER
all for what she
can geet
in Mi hour
of need
made Me feel
sharn DIVVET
in Mi faider's
own home
what would
You expect
from a
common limerick
God knows why
he thought her
rare as HAA
How easy
thae dolt
was swept
awa'

I cannae take the Doe
Eyes any longer
Whanev'r I turn
cottage corner
or quick sweep pew
I see You blaring
Whaurev'r I stand
Holes beget
Your eyes upon Me
Folks call it harmless
unwanted attention
stout convention
So I'll say I do
when I don't like
the scent of You
on Me after
a tied tight Night
Quick tae rid of Me
Mathair says I'll
Learn in time
tae love It
And soon enough
thon baby-sick
will replace
Your mace taste

Lord let me not
have a shotgun
wedding
Let there be at least
a few days
to put up the banns
before breech
of head through hole
Ma and Pa hold
the loaded Pistol
You There behind
counter courting
Did ruin her
Spark about eight months
ago pistol
Pointed one
Just couldn't
keep Your powder dry
until ring ready
Unknot wad shot
Blood clots lips of
A Violence protects Her
Honor but Your friends
hear near with own arms born
And poor Abbie
shot through
Died by morning light
Parting breath
Redden rips
Her hole honor
RESTOREN

Ah singing oot
across moors
peerieweerie
Nane could hear but
Thee
Sisterly QUITHER
Forget me nots
tug at blue thots
Speak the language
of flooers
feed
wet wean
single pointed healing
gleam teat
Whilockie thaim what traipse across acres for a frolic
Ah lown gloamin'
forelocks foretell
a bad Spell
What Pa presented
Ah couldna love There
Whaur future
silver coins drip
We bundled once
Ah rounded wame He
settled upon Her
luchts o' raven hair
Unknowing My condition
Nae rose relief
release His seed
dung doun
I pray
To grow wings that'll carry it
Ayont it's native speck o' grit
And Ye arrive!
before Ah've spoken bee
balm in hand
ready rip sheets
soak up fresh blood
wi' stale bread
Incantin' elixir
SorcererSister

His hands are
rough
robins egg
speckled
see silver
hairs glint as
He severely
squeezes
each teat
Young Tart
I bury
My shriek
before
the Elders
suspect me
Suspect of
bearing issue
Light into
World before
Matrimony
They seek the
single drop of
Milk that will
prove me
Depraved
Their lips
curl up
spittle
ends

Rue

Bring on the courses
Roux
Cook equal
flour to fat
raw flavor rendered through
Burning sap
Prevent pap
Yellow lace
Herb-of-grace
Hreowan
'make sorry
distress
grieve'
Erase every trace
Hreaw
Raw he had Me
Middle Dutch
Rouwen
Rowan tree under which
I bury
My sorrow
Rowing up stream
To lay
Repent
Ruddy berry
PIE root
'to push, strike'
Out—out
Rumination—
How old
Wid Ye've
Been now
had Ah
Let Ye
breathe

No mind to Marry
at present
Only just passed my
Needle-point test
And besides
Little wonder After
Our pent-up board
double dutch coupling
Close holes rubbed real
duchess hides & Seek
furrows fingers whet
lick teeming
Quest divine
ripe time
oh-so-quiet to flee
for a wee peak
Our soar-sought tryst
ghost-written
flea *bitten* up her New
Amsterdam west
without so much as a net
over midges the size of
My muff and You
Sweaty Huff
so swiftly entered
it was two shakes
of a lamb quake
and I all at stake
only left with
no O awe
tender scratch
bloody patch
on sheets of
sodden sand

Wynet Werth

Her *impulse from a vernal wood*
Begot hiss roaming hands Now what's her
worth once priceless Jewel Scratched sheets
of sodden sand Olwen's sharp in broken
light Time for accounting's come Pa wants
his fifty shekels due According to Good Book's
drum Marmsy do tell what Grammy knew Her
ravishment upbraids A maid taken in bush or brake
By absent rake must be paid Uneasy to prove Her
ravished THRU Her Light glows red in pane Perhaps
a firmer fichu might've Covered tempting cleft twain
Or longer petticoat might hide Bright hole's unholy seal
If we succeed in proving her Most worthy of a meal As
recompense she'll reel what Every forsaken lass is owed
A bull of three winters well-greased And shoved toward her
abode Bull tail buttered-up and shaven thrust Wide
through her skint door-clate And she to stand
on t'other side Her hands Abiding take
His tail strong if she could hold on
More dower to her And If it slips
through her fingertips Scratched
Ether benumbed strands All
what's left of him the seed
in Her groan hotshredded
B A N N S t h r e s h o l d
SPLITunderthings *and what*
grease may adhere to her hands

Where the mind is led forward by thee into ever-widening thought and action
Into that heaven of freedom, my Father, let my country awake.

Rise, like lions after slumber
In unvanquishable number!
Shake your chains to earth, like dew
In which sleep had befallen you
Ye are many—they are few!

/Rise, like lions after slumber/

In/
Quietude
dwelling
It
will not do
while
atrocities
mount
Her own
Conscience
Opens
The tent
Flap
What have I to
Offer

Offal
I Offer My
Body all
Its subtle
wonder
Every figging
plunder
The black
Pudding of it
However off
Putting
In/trails
Must be
Nourishing to
sum

What takes place
Out There
Shakes grace
In Here
To swallow
Their beating
My hard
Organ drips
pressed
against\
encasement

Seeming help
Less full of
volition
violence visited upon
Her scaled
smashed
broke
breeched
Inner hid in fear
By chamber pot flew
window wide guide
Down the hall choke
Which coat
Armed

I bumble
upon Your
bloodred
cap
in the image
You are standing
on those steep
marble steps
Rushing the whole
horned
Stop the
steel eyes
I cannot shake
Ask are
You a Patriot
And even before
You answer I
Who turn
Your worn wrist
shorn tryst
These cords
silken sour
can be used
as true Ties

I know a druid
Soul when I
flee one
a bed fleeced of
honey whet beard
the wheat won't be Gold
heat flounced down
Never love one
who keeps Thee
unfree

Thee
knot
Other
Thee
Ever lasting
Sublime
SNAIDHM
CHEILTEACH
Made of
Divine brine
Regenerative
Interweaving
Leaves lace
Plait the cord
Agency by which
Any body
Could be
Mother

You've heard
Tell
Know too well
The severing of
Mother
/from Beloved
Auctioning off
for skint coins
Our common
Divinity

'Ours are God
rearing steeple'
Meaning We keep
the piece
Wad shot
Up the tundra light
pernicious path
Night flight not
the same as
Egress by day
Whole fight bereft
What's left of
human chords

Mark My hoards
Are You a proud
Boy stand back
Unhand Me
hypovolemic
Understand red
wrong way Why

Pinned down I

Go beyond
My element

Seal up your lips and give no words

but mum.

While Ye
Test for purity
'Ye've no corset
Nothing tae keep
the girls up
t'wards
Sun'
And what do
Milk eyes aspire to
Yer
Breath like a badger
Belch like a bagpipe
And be chok'd if I don't
wish I could do the same,
for my wind-pipe is
furred like a flue

But a meek airy sprite
I keep mum and

Let Ye pass between
The drawbridge
Is closing
See Yerself
Out
Cannaye?

Shipbored life
'filthy bilge water'
gently bred daughter
white bread kneed
Talk smutty to Me
Who moves
Starboard
I can't make out
Your preachers
Claim purity
Hard core
Only own no God
But Mammon
Adamantine greed
must be
barmy to breed aboard
this clattering
Mad ship

In possession of

Little but

Her mind

What more could one want Really

Himself the timoneer?

You could point Your prow

By the smell of her kelp

A salted scent

him shoot shift up her

sheba sheath

Your vessel called

Shining Light

Sails straight O Arran

'kidney of the saints'

To be cleansed

Tune Your pipes and

fall ahumming strumming

oil rubbed

walrus pet

sudden swells

bravely met

Must stay barefoot fer

the boat of life

Trappings of the
Misguided
loath lily-white lesson
in the common lore
The Three Times
are ever incomplete
What passes for
Past
lacks the Brute
We seek
glisten over
Ancestral fields
fly imaging airy
But the night
soil retains carnivorous
Mind
mangles reel

Matter, My Father
stolen this
Fear and Awe
Joints tearing
the willow bark
Headaches
pulsed hot
rippling filled
tore through Her field
of vision
forage fennel for
the muscles and the wet

Maintain this abode
cracked peeling
Humble dwelling
S W E L Ling with weather
Whither we do
Depends upon the
Mere
Caprice
of
A woman who hasn't
Worked a day through
Never scrubbed the floor
till knees bleed
Unknown the pangs
of holey boots
rags-&-bones
pealing
Never bundled for wa'armth
need seeding union
Upper-crust fusions
Baked on greed
steep separate
bed chambers
landowners common
tufted toffs
scoff Our
Communal
scruffy trough

Of avenues and
Wildernesses
rare trees planted
in the Pleasure Grounds
bow woodlands to
Lady Nature's
Second husband
Oxygen was
discovered Here
capability browns
bluebells and narcissi
peering in pools beside Her
Doric temple folly
'If our Shell-born
Lady wants
Her lake There—
well then,
She'll have it!'
Just move Us yonder
wild harnesses
Hill hamlet
My erstwhile abode
Now charnel grounds
Your dryads must
Go in black gloves
Bury Our
heirless remains
in Sediment unruly
Spirits
bundle
Beneath Your
sinuous Swim

Squaring the lands
a troublesome tenant
'did not meet Your
Ladyship's approbation'
Walk sixty miles for
One word
Or I'll cut Yer oats
Lucky throats
Worked the land
For over a century
But they don't
Want Our bones now
Mud and sticks
bothán shakes
If ever pity was extended
Leave Me My little holding
An Gorta Mor
Say something in
My favor

Who pranced off
Horse Dancing
while We
dug for
grub
Plumed hats and
ringlets
to Our ringworm
How cavalier You
Look upon Our
Hunger game
with lace collared
Sublime disdain

Your history gets in the way of My memory

In Your absence You polished Me into the Enemy

Enter who All curse

Center her crown

Tower dower

yore in situ Now

Peacock head Ingleaming

'Trinket'—to gem—'Me to adorn—How—tell'—tonight?

Poet potent

like a third eye

fondseed

alluvial adornment

Legacy looting

Koh-i-noor

SIGN his hand

Duleep

young boy

Hands own yore not diamonds

for sand river sieved

Crave what Singh

Bequeaths priests

Empire Depraved

Dismayed how simple

common glass

round rings blue

Purpureal queen

setting which gem

Horrors fresh scoffing

Return never

And crown Her in
Blood gems from
Whose hands
plunder
And never return
Chaste chases cast
fount of hole Alluvial
Adorn bent
Fondseed
Like a third eye
potently Gleaming
in the head of peacock
Now sits in your dower tower
Crown Her center
Curse all who ENTER

Gaze *gauze*
        woven air
waving *water*
        eventide *dew*
Now a dead art
        Dacca Diaphanous
Pulled all six yards
        Through a ring
Gold Your
        Colonial
Years tore
        Thumbs
Weavers hands
        Mangled
dismantled
        Looms reticent
Raw cotton
        Shipped
Hungry island
        Nation
Degradation of
        Muslin today
So coarse
        Brays
Mechanical haze
        Past wonder
Her eyes
        Autumn dawn
Only then rays
        dew Airy
starched as
        Ring round
Ether   reel
        faerie

Dew-deft fingertips calling Home as the crow flies
Sailing her twine-tawny mist sewn as the crow flies

Alight bare muslin! azure Aurore that fabled hour
à vol d'oiseau mussing waves You comb as the crow flies

Foggy waters bleak You seek sweet Vanishing point
Raven-Floki radar-ready Om as the crow flies

Beheld her bright jewel bulging to be taken
Bloody Firangi mousse-mouth foam as the crow flies

Set to sail loam a cage of crows pecks out her eyes
All his plans biting blown as the crow flies

Sweet talk Me amorous rambler Ah don't desire
steady story— do roam Your tome as the crow flies

Raven on hill flaps silken smear wail wounded woods
Dear green, shake keen knifepoint moan as the crow flies

Her frisson of fear debtor's prison ever near
Meek body merely Here pawned groans as the crow flies

Death's at the door what are We waiting for Dear God
Is Gracious the world rapacious drone as the crow flies

Eldritch stare, Sorciere, I cannae discern for You
What is true from faux-gnome as the crow flies

Origins? rather wear tin than blood diamond
Is that red I see on white gown as the crow flies

Diaphanous dream Don't hide Your bride in veiled suites
Open up wide let God inside sown as the crow flies

Perhaps the same bird echoed through both of Us Yes
today *separate in evening* gloam as the crow flies

Bundling bodies fuse good morning wings Muse
And I Ether dissolve Your dawn-bone as the crow flies

Cloth like light

Vapors of dawn

Shimmer somewhere

Verandah

Thin top spin

Swelling to thicker

Ends

Handloom

Along the banks of

Meghna

Sprays

Boalee

Jawbone

yarn soaked flowing

Bengal

Translucent

Soft gossamer

cannot Transplant

Phuti Karpas

Silken sense

Motion hands

Memory tossed

Whose hands

Whose hands

Gond Beyond

Siren Song

O weaver whose seams

perfectly vanished

Muslin

mussin Our Muse in That fabled fabric
strummed by young sirens in azure hour mist supple
fingers subtle thrum moisten air by riverbanks on
moored boats Mermaids melody You wrap Me See-true
as sheer church glass Soft blown ventus textilis woven
wind light bind roll in from behind Thy bride might as
well clothe herself with a garment of the wind Clings
to her form and through Sun arrayed You see her whole
Venus at the altar Stand forth publicly naked under her
clouds of muslin eldritch mist mulls nothing as simple
pride & prejudice Maritime Silk Road Mousse foam
My mouth Your Ride & Rejoice Contrary to Cotton
logic Her fibers shrink instead of swelling in Mengha's
magic stream Shana 'reed comb' Boalee Jawbone
Abrawan 'flowing water' Habnam 'evening dew' Tanzeb
'ornament of body' Nayansukh 'pleasing to Eye' Mul
mul Bengali Bamboo bow Dhunkar Dunk Her in 'a
light raga' Heavy fibers low down rags silk rose hair
Mermaids mist Strumming Air ov'r cotton bundlin'
Light pulled UPward sung as You spin river shroaded
fog Where all thon weavers Gone ethereal Omen

A weaver wonders
over wool
Blankets can be
bundled for Beloved
Couple swaddled cold
Sunrise warmed by
Awakening Eyes
newborn Or Else
Doused in disease
For extinguishing
'unwanted' tribes
Manifest Your
merciless feast
He blew and they
Were scattered
To reduce the 'Heathens'
'Heaven's Ordinance'
Dip linen gift in contaminant
Unsee the sacred Mothers
Scars and blindness mute
Centuries of wisdom while
White lead covers Hers
A cult of reverence
'The Warrior Queen '
a pearl dangles over
Her hole impenetrable
while Her fingers caress
The Americas
An island nation aspires
Across Atlantic
Salvation comes
from Whose Suffering
by twist of
Mind's muscles
not the stitching
but what You do
with each thread of
gold may be spun

Good or ill—Heal or kill
Wherefore weave with
toil and care
The rich robes your
tyrants wear?
with this thread
Humbly freeing
I will wed
Fellow Feeling

You are Young
and You are Prettie
You are Single what
a Pittie
I am Single for your Sake
what a charming
for Me
Companion you would
Make

CELLACH 'bright-headed'
Learn Yer letters
in a hedge school
dodging wrens
who would peck out Our eyes
as soon as feed Tu
Suckling weeds
For sustenance
Her once fair
Green mouth blares
Uncared for
a famine orphan
in a bothán
burnt
trace letters in mud
'and always on the edge of survival'
swell with air belly
dawn sound of the workhouse bell
Máthair ballad
Böhland
Beóllán
Bow a bend in river
Polan rural person
Cannot dispel
This blight
Rotting mass
Graves appear everywhere
East of a holy well
Your breath on Me
'Faithful and bold'

Ballinanima

Ballingaddy

Elgin to Adelaide

And the quiet sweat of wax

on this veiled evening

Who knew my love would sail to Me
Upon

The Bee

A depth mined
Bobbin Lace
deft fingered Grace
earns her keep
where thread
is wound
a head for intricacy
adept mind
where thread
is hitched
rouse *réseau*
Hold on thread
Wood or bone
Until the
mechanical
Metal arm
Replaces
Your bones
and blood
pairs
tensioning
hands bound
supple subtlety
lacemaking
My only gift
fall out of fashion
spinning alms house
quickened qualms
Pass Me into Thee
PASSEMENTERIE

Ken them
whit has
evenae more
Mouths tae feed
Ah sought
To be
of Service
Beyond
Her own plaster
Walls but the
Cupboard hollows
tugboat bare
undercroft dry
coffers stitch together
Naething fer the Kirk
Regeneration
cracked blood
caked hands
Loch Me Wide
Sky Mind
SMAOINEACHADH
Mouths being
fed every
succulent delight
Forenicht on Nicht
May it be
sew

Dogtooth violets

in the dye-house

Myself

I like the indigo vats

Piecemeal pattern

passementerie

Whittled bone

condensery

Leave me peace

damned

Cold wet

Tapestry wool

Raw hands

Sans bands

Dog-tired

Better than Your

faux Silver lace

Churchgoers grace

Leg in the cupboard foreclosed her

bare mind

Our

babe could have been perfectly formed

drying of the Moon

Leave off Me Wandering

woods sylvan quill

COILLTE

quilted *caves*

illuminations

soul carer for a Mère aveugle

hell-mouths tomb

Rain squalls

purpureal runes

Clad in white
singing Peace
For kind and country
Bundled arm in arm
Sixty thousand of
Us 'tempestuous'
'animating'
Being powers
refuse to print
Our true
Marching calm
on Manchester
Mammary gland
of our Mothers
Instincts
Caroline ousted
stakes our votes
for a larger sliver of
the hand raised pie
crushed
Parliamentary Procedure
Silver slaughters women
children Trampled
upon Breast-like Hill
Ye are many—
They are few
Peterloo
Peterloo
fevered hues
Her dearest one
Only Two
slain
For what purpose
Cyclic pain

Let my sisters
prepare hair and
cakes in the hopes
of snagging a Swaddle
from some sappy Hymn

Wad away the years

whilst I see Self
muckle moor
than
barley bearer

A woman is not a field
to be continually
employed in bringing
forth or enlarging
grain

I may not be brawny
Six-foot tree

Or learned in machinations
as Mrs. Mason
muscular arms
match musculature of mind

'I know I have the Body but
of a weak and feeble woman;
but I have the heart and stomach of
a king'—

Cold, hard, Empirical
Eye? Ah
NO

female fripperies
Give Me shabby dress
without any stays to
            digress digesting

CALM MIND ABIDING

And the only ballad
I wish to sing—

Sacred hole powers—
Our Edible flowers

During her stay in Castle Joyous She misplaced her energies *sighing softly sore* soaring from room to room herself taut of *many beds for delight* Separated only by illumined screens She gazed and gazed lustily upon bodies heaving *in an enchanted mirror* a limb hacked across whose face unable to name holes nimbly used cum numbly sans a-kissing aplenty rods cold and thirsty sap tapestries fraught hot too wet to whet Only dessicate her Spiritcore Pleasure parched lonesome On her lap she clamped Head *no lenger there be stayd* Mud fallen *monument to sensuality* She must convert by Light of sudden sun heart sky wide Quaker-quick quicken wick Chaste 'severely simple' to produce a healthy fruit

Until rain began to
pelt down
You hadn't noticed
the roof
needed patching
arms above head
daub with clay
a hole the size
of her heart
enlarged
emitting sky
drippings
Would keep You
Wet through
Expectancy
Even in
Your condition
melon round
He refuses
no longer courting
to plug
drunk skunk
on the mead
Wonder what
You first saw
in Him
Bundling back when
You tiptoe up
rickety stool
Slipping upon
fast gathering pool
and out slips
the unfinished babe
You'd long carried
this loss repercussive
sudden hollow belle
In court they
name You

Witch
chant
Lock Her up!
Back home
lay open
the roof continues
to tear
Her gaping wound
bare

Old cottage collywobbles
sprout dirt
kicks up the hearth
more often than not
Mud on toast
but I don't
Envy the ship
Captains their houses
made of brick
leaded glass
Widow towers
where no Wisdom keeps watch
Truly I know what is brought
along those hallowed routes
Going down
to Underworld
and never really returning
every scintillating coin
They touch a plunder
Tinged with soulful
Human blood

There is no safe
Harbor no
Refuge to take
Out There
Our pearly North lies
Just as tied
Ship side
Sailing brazen
in a bevy
of bloody knots
cotton cords
umbilically torn
Coddle
We make in
Love bundling
Two together
as if sacred
can be preserved
Sweetening up the
Berry-Bleeding horizon
When the world's
a Devil riding
Hell slide
the mind slips
in happy swill
savior Conscience
Upbraiding knots
How brightly we
fancy Ourselves
Abolitionists
Fancy Ourselves
Full stop

Beware the Adze
of March
Midway midwife
a free state
gives birth to
a new Union
Anemic pines
steady timbre
By two votes free
Tempers rise
Like a fire bell
amber dart
Low down demon
may kill
Lovejoy
Toss press terror
in missing sipping
river but They
won't kill Our Free
We meet in Emily's
Parlor poems shake
I shall never forsake
Our cause
sprinkled in blood
Away runs night
Albion
knell of the
Hushed indeed
Hold me here bundled tight
where tundra Light
is freer still
Down is up
Here

Holier than Thou
Her suffrage abolition
Know no bounds
But the cloth
across her dainty nape
binds from Below
clotted cotton
in blood lit chains
and the weave
that wafts her grace
floral to conceive
by tiny hands
in dank mill
Cough it up
downy dregs
way up here
there is no
Holy state
as long as
He profits
All is taint

You've seen the
Country now
You know the
undertow
excites the turn
in road
sew seed in
-seminate
Land of the free
They're giving it
Away
Tear thickens
blood quickens
Your pace repast
Gorge on *When*
does the Present
become the Past
No shelter from
What's to come

They'll milk her

till they take a

hammer to her

Then you'll have

blood pudding

for your dinner

Beira yields
farmland whore
SILE
Tilled by the Oat Father
Noo understood
Grown not flown
Humble oat
Regenerative cloutie
feeds Our need

OCH fertile fields of Fife
Give up Your Bounty

Digde yields
Cow-witch
Fire feast
CAILLEACH FEASA
with a cloak and a veil
Ah made Me own
Groat milk fur them
what Rounded in Me
chafing feed
Weans bite
thon teat what
Bleeds

Draining Loch Spynie
No wonderin' whither
Dug by hand caterpillar
canal creeps
spine above sea
Future ken
Frae that peak
judge us bleak
for emptying depths
Our lost lochs
Lossiemouth
EUTROPHY green
alder swamp
slenderleaf
pondweed little
greb no moor
spread seed o'er
lady landers o'
Mystic power

Inversnaid

Let them be left

I'll not to market

Love offering

every good thing

for their plumping

out tender touch

He takes them

to their death

Not an ounce

of flesh

crosses my lips

I eat green

whisps of light

He suckles

from the belt of blood

the Wounded Stag melts

the Eternal Bard

with her fáawn-fróth

hole

I cannae watch while

He croons Gaelic

killing

everything that moves

pine martens

golden eagles

Corresponding

passion for plants

passion for blasting

anything that mothers

what possesses
He nourishes

His daft fleurs
from the loch sea kelp

a splash of His help

pink Orbs grow showy whilst
He blows anyone in sight

Then Wonders why

Bare heathpack Echoes Back

NONE left to hunt

dichotomous plight
of this being

in bed with the
One who exterminates

by rifle by knife

What agency

If I could shake free
All pulsing sentient life

Let them be left

O let them be left,
wildness and wet

Long live the weeds
and the wilderness yet

When I walk in the greenwood, a shudder I feel
As near as the shadow that lags at my heel.

The flower petals flitchered and flamed wi'a hiss.
Far, far in the past, yet alive is this bliss.

/Degged with dew, dappled with dew/Are the groins of the braes that the brook treads through/

You know this Land
like the back of My hand
places mossy and
impassable
continuously exhale
lacy wings light up
Yon night frolics
and the dell
where blue bells
wring out Your
need for freeing
upbraid who when the
grass sullens
once wet rooks find
other nooks to
bathe the foxes
leave dens for
fairer suppler glens
I feel this drought
like my own parching
Pen seeing is a
Magic shiver east
Her lilies quiver burn up
Green hope ends
Before wilting
She's given so much
from her teat the
gods did suck
Now Danu needs
Our loving care

Water-mother, Air lass
consider
how to be, which way to live
to carry the heather
spread it
work wisdom
trickling mead
study the stars
as little nests
born from your kneecap
born alone from your
lonesome days
set free quietude
a womb full of
waves
Spawner
hidden reefs
shape the bays

To fill with milk
honey from the heather
not blood from spry
feather
She is porous
the rate of decaying
Truth
Refresh the Muse
at the purespring
Fragments of My
petite épopée
position Your quill
against Mother
nature You will
always lose
You may as well
work with Her
stamper away
surveying His
shore-roads
As if land
could be owned
But Earth
giving what She
has to offer
Hold blood
Your spilling
a little longer

Sugar dusting the First
Green sprigs
Sudden as Snowdonia
rushing in
federbed feeling
for you
cozy up
on slopes below
the wettest spot
Eagle Abode
Slate mind be damned
mining for copper
mill ruins reek
You seek the rare
Snowdon Lily
Arctic burst of Sun
Beware the seven year
fungus on *Eyryi*
Where waterfall so clear
daffodils appear
to be dancing
desolate fiddler
where She leapt
Our dreams wept

HIRAETH

Hearth heareth

High wraith

Here etched in

E'm Longing for

Home

Chasing

There is no

More moor

Ah never knew

What a well was

What well was till

Empty

run dry

Wandering tomb

of Womb

What You Attend to

Grows

Memory herder

hoard her

can't go

Home This land

not My own

Seek after

Our being in

Womb float

What sunsets We suckled

Clouds particular

to that nip

of coast

How high the waters rose

mountainous robes

surviving churches thrown

over parched farmland

where up tree

perish for want of succour

Wild irises

pour ash

pucker

Home sick

Firecloudfish

throat stuck

suck her

rutted Wheel

chasing Afterglow

gutted

Her mind
enclosed by
High bare hills
Shepherd
Local lore
Bore your
Redolent
Roman road
Covered over
Asphodel
Ghost village
creaks in the gale
Construct a
permanent
Farm way
Where you
Can dip
down dales
straight on
sheep
the suture
steep
the future
to hold inside
Her vast
Knowing
Bear Your hills high
so He can enter
in the Center
Ring on the rim
diaphanous
He'll find Your
Emptiness
Womb of
Compassion

It all started
in a Garden

None can get at Me *here*

Refuge We built
of roses
redolent rambling climbers

Scotch arouses coverlet

Scots briar vines taut part

pine of bed hammock
Bundling wings

moth mouths Light beating
Let's stay in here
Paradise
Who'll say
Why have You let
the Garden Run Wild

Only observe Her
Not disciplined
No measure
A pleasure to watch
Grow at liberty
fecund flow-her

profusely for a
short shot

Bee dips
Inner slope
Just free

WNCO MWNCO

oon-core moon-core

'him over there'

Home over where

Moonlight lamps

His lovesaking eyes

shaking flies off her

Cuckoo clamps

Woodpecker

Voice become one

with woodland sound

ONCO FONCO

oncore von-core

'her over there'

Encore trap door

Knocked up on

limbs of oak hoar

frost rooms You led Me

through all for a

quick CWTCH

catch cuddle fond

LING DI LONG

Hold on strong

carefree

joined without

rings

betrothal springs

PILI PALA flight

Blue balls

flutter ring

MoonCore

No matter how poor
You can give

sunsets   sunrises
when you get them

imprint mind aura
what we're chasing

loch hopping
thick foggy moor

antennae taut
was sleep

made of butterfly
net

We were caught
winging

sodden fog
clears

skyily I offer
this

auroral vision
sudden scion spells

blue wing woosh
boundless Beings

Young You never
Wondered
What was it that
captivated So
Them panting uphill
a weird spirit
a rainbow from end to end
the body tying
across the fells
to guide themselves
Now with only
a pair of old boots
and a scruffy muff
not kitted but knitting
the road close together
Our paces matched
mellifluous
heading up
look at that shaft
of sunlight
Golly godly

Cairns like this one
adding a stone
as You pass
Help You stick to
The Path
in thick
eldritch mist
You see the peak
Nearly beside it
Calm Waters
When a sharp
stinging resounds
What bit wonders
Ease the muscle
by expanding
the breath
tossing your
warm-held Find
golden Rind
for others
Beyond You

Fondness for this fell
between the deep hollow
nestled on the edge
bracken covered
Haystacks where We
fond of a cuddle
buttered Your
Buttermere
Made a mère of You
butter lake
sink your teeth in
good pastureland
tarns *tjorn* teardrop
views into the
valley below
Mellifluous!
DIVE IN
part the water
Lakelands
Our communication
echoes down the
decades
in every fleshbreath
ripples kiss

Misusing the
Wilds
great swarms of
folk midges
gabble and gamble
about Her fells
utterly
missing that
solitary quality

A gentle generous
chap
engages brain
before opening
mouth trap
lips
endearingly
enter
landscape
to savor
Her hills
hummocks
honeyed Sweet
Part take
what's There

Follow the light by her V
Venus
Folding star

All the shepherds

Into the fold

Towards the owlet light

Load star (lodestar)

Your light in her

Explodes

A wanderer, He
will always Find
the Blue heron

A wonderer, I
where You lead
Fly My blue plume
blinking

DUNTER

Duck duck

Duck Here

Where eiders abound

You need only follow

She is *emsket*

blue gray mist

He is dichotomy

embody

gruelly bag

light green plumage

on nape of Du

Eider faces a huge

Swelling

AIDER WHY WHOW

wave crest

dive right in

plumes the depths

emerge Other side

Sure she can't fiddan

a dee with bow

or abandon!

widna laek ta

bide

backaboot

place

rest

fine layer

under tougher

she plucks off her

heather gray chest

feed her nest

small interlocking

threads clump

air pockets

to keep her eggs

and wee warm

An times whin darkness

niver faas

idda Laand

o da Simmer Dim

Night is ever agloaming

Farm her Sanctuary

Keep away Aider

rogue tongue

STOP the muncher

muncher munchers

mink fox

can't catch

roaming free

her wings

unscathed unkilt

Our bed to be

built down rays

Praise her quill-t

snugglin haze

For mine ether duck

I thee drake

And by my wild gaze

I thee gander

Behold

Delight Be here

with Yourself

on dry land

broad-leaved

Coniferous woods

Scots pine

Domed drey of twigs

In a branch fork

Tree hollows

Lay leaves moss

Scarce berry hid here

MATING in late winter

Your red squirrel

Gets up

Lord knows

Mischief

Murmurs

Beau slow

blow slow

You only savour

First fruits

once

Be holed

Shetland flock
Rubbed fleece down
Plant Your
shelter belt
Make seed known
crofts abound
common grazing
muck in
winter
grass is poor
verdure throbs when
first sheep to taste
tips of
winterwheat
winterbarley
stunt growth
just enough
steady hips for
Spring

Finish the font
concerning the heavenly
Arrivals
before it's too
Soon
Forsythia sprigs
golden tune
blasts through
I spring up
weeping
loss of it
bedding Down no
longer requisite
Forsythia signals
the beginningless end
Spring bed distends
with humid brays
with humid brays
All hands to the
Field to Plumb
Sow Yield
Her till she
bestows
Sudden distant memory
You tickling My
fuzzy udder
in milk white winter
I milk that suckle
Here when
Summer's sweaty swoon
takes You away
from nuzzling In
Swaths of muslin Your
Hard wood
board Will be stored
Till colder climbs
Back Her
hearth Holed up
make no
inner dew till
Soily Then

Call me forth

When Eden is done

Freya's forsythia

Gilt slit dips

Green emanations

speak deep

BELTANE

Buds milk Myself

of a feeling

the sound

of cloth

ripping

Open

Lick your finger

then touch her fold

Sheela

Crocus

was very old

a ghost

Look!

Purpureal

Verdure of the New

Neid fire

Swelling bee

Spirit

pussy willow

windblown We

rotate under

Walpurga

cloaked

her falcon feathers

SacralMoon

Brísingamen

each ribbon

one wish

Dance round You

Maypole

Birch Rowan Hawthorn

My polestar glows

Teineigen

Jack in the Green

Lech chases

Maids bearing

May blossoms buoy bosoms

hornyThe Need Fire

OH Aye

Whack

Key to leafy briar

We thwack him dead

Pull leaves for luck

The killing of a Tree Spirit

Regeneration

glittering chitterlings

Your sacred boar

Hildisvíni

Jump flames

Far to purify

Let's Us couple

creaming May

Obby Oss

Overfire

Future feck

flames lick slit

sparkseedlings

Until It

Tired of

mouldering

set Me

Library alit

out'n da glen

fair all ta see

Spirits uneasy

Thon gale

made book

covers flap as

loony sound

barmy down

Lapwings

teuchit(s')-storm peewit green fllopwing

March mad

tap spring

breed in

eternal

pairs

acrobatic

clown courtship

flairs

Yon Sky

gaggle of

glee

Romance often flowers
in the dirt
All that glistens
Ripples the frisson
Handling seeds be Fore
Each Other
A prelude played
To Mother

A lark's tongue lured
Your inner shoot
His beard shook
lumbered about
the pines
dashing past
airy swamp
the stench of which
this country
foal flings
the wide open glades
wobbly muscles
learn to hold
the road
of bird cherries
awakes Quake
Her flaming parrot
fringe ruffled
tulips lurid red
one strong stump
broadly bled
Her bare

Gentle steed
Been broken in
mere Mare
fleabitten
No one wants
to plant his Seed
Where another man's been
Only You
Took me on the
Open road
the Moors glowed
la Mer unbowed
as We rode Home

Indelicacy
Reared properly
Horse flesh
He has been so
initiated
'Nice gentle mares'
Galloping wild
Canter cantos
Not God fearing
Goddess hearing
Amateur riders
fall not When
I rode You
the snow
seemed to be
glowing Upward

The wilds
in His mother
required some trimming
She would
rapture the rending
apart of
God's architecture
Come only recently
to this left behind place
where elders continually squeeze
Milk might betray her
Marrow man
debating intricacies in
the Word
mind fodder
reign in
folded fields seed
I'll wild wed
All aboard bride
Broad new world
Antinomian
Nomad

Better be goin'
while the tide's

still with Us

Townmind

wouldn't know
a riptide from

a raindrop

Mist on water

cleared
The Isles

lit up
fern-green

Meagre home
made of beach and sea

Thanks be
myriad Dryads

I prepared for Ye
a meal of see-weed

over driftwood
Don't ask me

to wad
on land

The Sea's in
Me blood

PERIPLUM
pearly plum
'parapluie'

This here heather
prepared far
any weather
but the Wadding
Nicht has Me fair fricht
WHA remedy
Get Yer Eye Up
Vantage point
frae the crow's nest
sea board seen
by men sail-ing
Saline spray
Her mouth
Cartography in situ
How land looks
swirling
from Yer Point at sea
Turn it round
Upside down
Befuddler HOLE
Thar' she blows
Still she grows
Further awa'
flichtery melody

Ye can't   read a map
for This Here peak

Look if Ye like
but Ye'll   *have tae leak!*

Ascent from
Gatesgarth
This mystery character
Have You seen
Many along the way
caught unawares
sudden burst of rain
or low mist creeping in
as if fairies weeping
Slow and pace
gently up the slope
I'm really looking forward to
getting to the top
to find out why
the view's so dear
Way up Here
Heard rainbows glow
symphonic streams
assuming We
Make It
That is

With You I trod
Bracken steeps
prelude of much
Merit
take a Peak
between valley cheeks
Your saddle nestled
mountains
crag overhanging
clear view of the
Climb unabashed
into the rhythm
roaming the gloaming
Match My steps with
Naked Awareness
Inner tunnel exit Her
Skyey sensory
Not arising not Arising
Rising and not arising
rising knot Arising
and knot Arising
and rising R
I
S
I
N
G
RISE
SING

O wild West wind, thou breath of Autumn's being,
Thou from whose unseen presence the leaves dead
Are driven, like ghosts from an enchanter freeing

Knocking from within barn walls Spirits saying,
we, too, lived with unmet needs
we, too, need attention

no such thing as invalid excursion
inhabitants of
the graves knocking on themselves

as doors

salt the moving outline

all the way back to the house

Must lie outside the house

Side of space I must cross

To write against the Ghost

/I also have heard the speech of many spirits/ at once,/ undulating like a scroll/

This farm where we grow
Our deep
And bundle under Sleep
These cracked walls
Where the mice
rustle
built upon it
Not Our own
There are gate keepers
land bearers We
Took what wasn't Ours
and now
The Spirits
Restless wrestle do
You Hear

Ouija chord talking board Your Yes withered honey and
the bee for Thee be with Salt above Water if My drips a
river River riding stick river bed spreads where too close
too far with His wet will ridden written on the charred
sweet Word *Oui* We inject into Her loose body hid
in ossuary thrust the pages in Your numinous
heart sense each other's heat and I this ram-
pant January am not quiet Ghost

Day begins at Dusk

Darkling husk

fumbled

found

Her round
Autumn belly

pump kin hind

fecund feminna

Carve a turnip

for Stingy Jack

mound Suckling

forced to roam

The Gloaming

Sum

SAMHAIN

Veil between

One and Another

Thin lace

Aos Si

I see Ye fairies

Bonfires lit for

Purify

Hollowed hallow

Verdancy eyes flicker

What deeds We did

Seed now in quiet

Mother gone beyond

bones

flowering bestows

Crisp

minal light

spire

spice rind

who groans

crones

pooling

seed

Autumn wed Our Tru

Bells gather Sealed neath

SHANNACH

Leaves Gong

long

Lacuna

Who goes There

murmuring in

Gossamer Floss

Otherworldly

Are Ye

Second Sight

Our "Reverend"

combs these Woods

First Sunday of every

Up Doon Hill

waking the twigs

for fairie sprites

ALIGHT on damp ground

His REVERANT ear to the

IN-visible

Fiery Faye Ether Real

How they live amongst

Your spectral double

secretes His secret beneath a full Moon

luminous numinous

Commonwealth

Of Elves Fauns Fairies

Body lies or does it

catches Us

Bundling in the

Leaves cocoon Our

spinning fast

rump to ring

about to wing

when His

Body leaves

Taken by fairies

He was

the one

Minister's Pine

among forest

of oak

Lone stalwart barking
We wrap in
many fronded
Rainbow body
silk cloth
prayers fraying

May all Yer

FAYE wishes

Be effortlessly
Granted

Beneath the roots
Ancient Tree shake
I the lone pine
in Oakwoods quake

Your subtle seed in Me
Enchanted

What is it?

Maids with heavy strides

All to forest

Where no light gets in but

Soaking moonlight

Little stars

staring through the leaves

It being the ole mid-summer
Eve

Bathed in Moon milk

Veil owre marrow

Round orbs

Bevy of maidens

Turned into the wood

Attempt some Spell or Enchantment

Pulse Moon upon her Visage

sowing hemp-seed

cream clotting

The proposed Peep *into Futurity*

Fuggy-hole

Before the moon rose

That reposeful time

funereal figures

in low tones

The dark side of the same holly

'Earth My body Water My blood'

Who will be My Love

Noces-fúnebres
j'enterrerai

Glided on her path
Whose fluttering gowns soon became visible

'Air My breath & Fire My spirit'

Bundle back home-along like hares

The larries flit

The moon whitening her hot

Blush away

'These Siths or Fairies

They call *Sleagh Maith*

or the Good People . . .

said to be of

Middle Nature

Between

Man *and Angel,*

as were Daemons thought to be *of old;*

of intelligent fluidous Spirits, *and light changeable bodies*

(lyke those called Astral) *somewhat of the nature of* *a condensed cloud,*

and best seen *in twilight. These bodies be so pliable*

through the sublety of Spirits *that agitate them,*

that they can make them

appear or disappear *at Pleasure.'*

Tuatha De Danān

'thoo a du-non'

True I do Anon of the Goddess 'muff' thus born Cave fairies come down clouds Heady banish your Magic first snaked in Skilled in 'Sweet-bottom grass' Dwelling In Otherworldly wags a poisonous I burnt ships smoke and mist down from the heaven orbs Spell over silver limbs '*ault fri halt dí & féith fri féth*' I will Him to regenerate joint to joint and sinew to sinew Invisible world sew evoke Bards record history flesh from flesh sounds familiar 'good hare finder' Brigid records herstory 'Breasts be dun' Cycle clasps Craft battles healer un-reads The barred book aloud Gold wires growing over Plentiful magic shroud True after all Origins do not cease post breath death a scented Cross stole lands The Great Caves of the Hills Above and beyond Mother Underground into a sinewy Sidhe Shee mounds 'Round rising hillocks' Onto a flowery plain of Honey what became of Them extinguished distinguishes whether Our crops be fecund erect redolent rot Remains roaring aural unravel

Ha none of Your

Roseate fay fairies

playing faun

doun da coast

Up har HAARY haggerin'

Our Fiery fairies breathe fire

burnnae caldroun

Fier comme un Ecossais

burnt thistle hair

Trees tufts and falty-flyer

All fear Her feelings

HEAVY-HEARTIT

Unrelinquished

Under an ETERIE Sky

Unforgivin'

An Ah for an Ah

O'speerit

Eat her tits raw

I dinna blame her fur't

ROOKY swoon

She is coorse catchin'

Thon loupin' wean

blood petaling

on ragged wings

You went to the Seer
To see Her ignite
Something in You
Which was departed
An emblem of bronze
Folded layers blest
Crest more faithful than
A ghost your aural folds
wet with/
Precognition invades
Intuition
Touch hymn
on any side surmount
Making sermon come
cannot
thrust their fingers In
Stabilize the stab
Mother Night
pervades My hero to
inflame or
mutilate Herself?
Exogamy

Tea leaf readin'

I see Yer

Hollow WEAN

Cusp dangles rottin' gourd

Hallowe'en

Between this world

And the Next Samhain

I weep for Your future loss

Choose not to lift

Thin veil o'er My

Blink away

Grey eyes wild

through lace wing

Because I would not let Him

Enter Me

Spit in My Mouth

teller unfortunate

If a priestess

Κασάνδρα cursed to utter

True prophecy

And never be believed

'All lightning ever wants to do

is strike Earth'

muffle mouth Her

hysteria of the

Feminine Divine

Mind thon belching

Steel rails faye fields

Skint wetland sudden dry

fireclouds floodshrouds

bees abscond No honey

for bitter

tea

'roof of the mouth'

I see it all

Beira's thrall unpalatable

Bottoms up Our cup

lick royal jelly from my

Otherworld utter

If a priestess

Never be leaved

Witchy day

Rain pelts

frae bark roost

wind Up whirligig

Gold birds

Crown round

Cerridwen's cauldron

mossy head

drumming

alight

Bound to fall boundin' awa' frae

What held them on

Sae lang

Me witch's teat

Cold

through

Hear that sap in veins of trees

shrinking

Me own need

of thatched hurdles

and boughs

build

a fire

over which a kettle SINGS

To be with the leaves
as they spring
off branch
One last dance
gold toed
Fire bodied

Hold that
Flight stance before
Their departing dance

A last drawn breath
ragged blithe
Woodsmoke
wafts across
top of
You elm
Orange dome
pearl mist owre
a kiss
from spirits
afore

Do you fear
the Spirits
Out My
pitch
window
stone foot
slipping
Hear the
Owl
vigiling
Angels
charge
keep
Thee
bundled
staid
all
Thy
Ways

Divine

Presence

Her fairy feat

danced off toes hole soles

leithbragan

because the spirit always making or mending a single shoe

ELPHIN

Were active there

Elf-lock

'knot of hair'

Mossy grotto

Plural

Elven

Feminine

Elfenna

Your hungry peat

compare

playful sprite

ælfadl

'nightmare'

So rare to

Meet someone

Who admires

One's treasures

rubbing back

Your

ælfsogoða

'hiccup' untame wind

You unmind My

See-Through veil

ylfe

'Incubus'

Misconstrue Midsummer Eve

Faeries

steal beauty

full *mortals*

for their brides

for the love of

Singing

Many a poor girl

Pined away and died

No fairy funerals Ire fiery tunes
upon
clumsy mortal lips inspire
fairy darts *dead cattle* *fairy rath*

and the pooka is abroad

Queen
Mab

Arise
incision
Ears
Single
Point
This numbing November Eve

Set the table with food
in the name of the devil

fetch of your lover *may come through window*

Yet instead met

Evil hob
Goblin

Gold lock
More noble

which it was not *Fortunate to dis-*

Entangle

ABER KNOT
Ah wished to make fer Us
An ornament of
Stainless Light
A mystical knot
on a wrestin treed
HESP
with three strands
Such a knot
a ready vessel
dwellin empowerments
Applied to a sprain
Grant to me
the prescribed
Incantations
in water script
wind-energies
succored up her
MERMAID'S GLOVE
HUMEN twilight trove
Root Higher Insight
HUSH HERTSHOT
Infallible remedy

Elphin grot
She brought Me
meet always in the
same place
flowerborder
sheets against
trunk of
My fur
crazing courtesies
true secrete
I love Thee
who on his
feet wild a-shriek
sloping roof
wooden pens
raising down
dovcoot

Coo O
won Ye
Take Me
            Tae
Shaky Toun
rocky outcrop
AM BAILE
CRITHEANACH
            Comrie
Tremors
            Squeeze
My hand
felt owre much
            for a
Full six minutes
such subtle Instrument
            Tae measure
Smirr
Her quaking
            Pleasure
'tossed on his bed
as he had never been
tossed out at sea'
            Salty drizzler
Lick waves
            sated fissure
Heidy seizure
            No knead
Seismometer

Parsimony
to be merry the
night through
without need
of candle tallow
There're fairer freer
Ways to entertain
Delicious Spark
Succulence
Questing across
The fairy filled
Fields arousing
My door
left upon the latch
by window way
or crackle stable You
stealthily enter
To bed Her
Don't blether about
A sable word or two
will do
Beg leave
pull off
upper garment
Grant You
lift up starry quilt
stealth spirit
Cum upon
The bed to
Her

Where are You Then
More delicious than
Dangerous
for a lad
the Tarrying
Alive he is booted
Out only if she
does Emit consequence
Controls who's fecund in flock
When squeezed hard
made me feel
Farmyard
a gutting
flash of the Spirit
and I've a mind for
mining pages subtler
nooks my body never
clean again Their hands
Their hands Elders ever
wrenching a ripe tart
You can see how
No forgiven for
Run as fast as
My GhostSour fruit
Brood Fairie
Forevermore Haunt this
fiery Wood

Cloaked herself next
Mourning for the undertaking

Reticent Reluctance

Release Me from this

Bond
My hands bound
in gold round

It do wherrit me terribly

Face once beloved now afeared

If You only knew how he do
Chevy Me round the chimmer
I shall die o' the thought
O that paper I signed
with My holy cross
Sign of the Slag

'Ch war always so rackless!
The far-off seems near
in My dreams
You'd pity Me
appearance of the woodlander

Meet same End
'ee when the breath's out
O' Your body
My
mind afterglow
I gave him
Can You save
Poor
woman's Skellington
from the ~~Heathen's~~ chopper
Dig her

Proper befitting

~~Christian~~ grave

She had furs to bring
the Lasses torn
tartan shorn
up the heath
fine heathered
Said a bad word
the brown beer
brewed willing
a Vision
backwoodsful burning
Your own daughter
Drink up Dear
Never fear
Farmind will save Her

If all the walls
be burning
and He
Farmind
comes In to
salvage what
fingertips
Father clubbed
Once a woodsman
held an ax
at my top
Sinews-ends
Douse Yourself
to save Your mind
Made of body
Made of mind

Now I'm not houseproud but
Take a little care
rumpled bed deadhead
nipples aching
from Our wee loss
Apply the salve
My own mind
I watch for
feet were cold
beside walls made of
Holes head winds
Bad spirits astir the
Night beclouded by
Bed blight
middlemost house
moist with mock boughs
uninvited glades
But in stories
between the bedpost
and My cloven limbs
He knitted
Ageless Abodes

History's hazelraw

How-dumb-deid

Let the untended

Stanes tumble

eemis weans

so's I couldna read

the names cut oot i' the stane

'yont yowdowndrift

Raking owre the past

Useless

Let the leaves

Fall where they lay

yirdit

mouldering

Gold graves

Careless free

Fug lang syne

Crowdieknowe

Unco Crow knows

Candor full CAULD

HAIRST NICHT

Whase coal eye

Begets the

Dew glade

Grass blade

This land not My own

wagging tongues

grips signs words

I hunger

And seek after

Home

Slips awa'

in ELDRITCH mist

Our tryst

'hideous, ghastly,

weird'

Elphrish

Uncertain origin

Clotted cream Moon

Former selves coupling

Ghosts gone Beyond

mating in *and with*

'else' *&* *ether*

'realm'

What lurks

Gut lurch

Bare limbed trees gleam

aprons beading

Masonic Mist thick as thieves

I sweat

Air wet with *Spirit*

Hard possible

If through mist mind

a trunk I perceive

Rub the Root

of Your

Malted shaft
yonder cherished mate
dripping dwellings
coarser was Her
Enterer stream steams
wade in wonder
We rump chanting
His knee drizzles over
And slashed
the dragon blood-drop
barely salted Her tongue
before the tree born
birds began to
presage
A hundred bearers of horns
A thousand udder-bringers
Would tear down the
piecemeal construction
What were You to Do
Now You know
brace Yourself
tense Yourself
fence Yourself
IN

Spinning-wheel was
Your mother
Banned her man
'Spin the yarn yourself'
No coddling
If You want a cover
to cuddle under
Grab that Innocent
and sheer
'warp-thread'
'reed-teeth'
'Down of a summer ewe'
'Listen now while I'm talking to'
Place wool in ears
Mother May I hear
The Green Goddess near
Turn the wheel of
the Tongue
flicking clouds

I Cannae cum to bed board till she's free of If only I could take Her
to Loch Maree perceived Queen V Thon Wishing Tree surely would
cure what ails biting eels of Her Mind *Muc-Sheilch* Here at the
Eye of the Loch I will tie her down in sacred waters heal Hermitage
Applecross Isle of Maree Chapel believed to be all manner of
Sacrifice what good druid daughter wouldn't brave to save
Woodsy isles riddled with Black Throated Divers Dragonflies
viridescent wings dart Saint Máelrubai from Isle of Skye
Arrive once bespoke Loch Ewe full on savor Caledonian
pine wood Oak Wish Tree holly Holy Mother Make a
sacrifice for *Muc-sheilch* Your own monsters pining away
lining My own womb lurks underwater post part them
Turtle-pig or biting Eel Eye of the Loch Turn the
key Wrists Bound with a rope Rowed round the is
Three Times and dunked shock into the Brisk Loc
Three Times and made to drink at the Base of
the Holy Well Three Sips and hammer Three
Coins in the bark till eons distill viridescent
nubs and cut Three Slits off Her garb
Strip of Cloth You see Contains
the madness and wrapping
round the Holy Bark I
transfer Her Dark Mind
into pine The Money
Tree takes on Your
sick SHAKES Now
withered poor tree
Where He built
His None can
Save Her

. . . Far over the woods,
Toll the world to thy chantry;
Sing to the bats' sleek sisterhoods
Full complines with gallantry:

Where the bee sucks, there suck I:
In a cowslip's bell I lie;
There I couch when owls do cry.
On the bat's back I do fly
After summer merrily.
Merrily, merrily shall I live now
Under the blossom that hangs on the bough.

/Then owls and bats, cowls and twats,/

Our cave was dim
Going in-In
No matter
Eye valley
expands till You blur
Water Her
bats
Regenerate broad light
Day has no equal but Night
Single Point
Concentrate
Hold on tight
Tickles it
Baby roaches up My
wrist
crumbs kissed
sense our tryst

Morning mouth
sour cerises
hair frayed
a kneady ball
Can I before
You rise
Rinse the whole
taut eyes
very scant sleep
nerves abuzz
honey sweat Yet
Awakener than ever

Opening off It
without
Constraint
allowed a very
farmyard scent
to emit
from Her chamber
Constant
punching churning
Shaking
down
Kiss me once, Eider
a good airing to
keep It fresh

Twat that forest clearing slit cut down the middle þveit the sea creature speaks in tongues one could not expect to comprehend is hungry appetites unbefitting for the fairer And Yet here whet rubbed round emit a haunting sound *Then owls and bats Cowls and twats* ink blots poet in habit Italia where lemons drip down sunny orbs coupling cover Our Beloved Aurora while away many a jocund hour above her exploring shimmerfur South once We were happily Away drouth misconstrue the redolent view for renunciate *as soon an Old Nuns Twat* sage to speak of what was given up for God Her value attached to Her Hole or fallen woman dishonoring her young nation seduced away from her station what recompense for illegitimacy a bastard catch'd by the severe edict of society the fairer the weaker the dainty *'not troubled (happily for them) with sexual feelings of any kind'* while we all know Pillocks to be full of licence unrestrained go into any clearing any time of day what are they looking for in the empty dank light tread pulping the woods hardcover booklover be seeking My O part that Clef fur shimmers ground cover (w)hole My where You come from where You are sewing

So we go
Commando
groaning chair
allowing air
to freshly move
Down there
Thon
access
undulates
undelayed
no frayed
cage for
fumbling
Yonder bumble-broth
Laddie,
Just part
diaphanous
muslin curtain
muss skin
Come
Ben

Clove scented water
for a soak
holiday activity
rubbed directly
Below stairs
Purify this
hot stones
self-pollution
drop In
hand upon
spiced with
Pleasuring
cinnamon cumin
might
My splashing dip
Go blind
minted fur
Was happening

There

Poor Piano
is out of tune
sings all slanted
as midwinter light
The Moon was
    New
But Love was
    Old
Auroral Night
tainted seeds
Many moons cold
since We've
enough food
from fields
A good brute
Boot wouldn't
Go amiss Here
You pump
the pedal
tenderly Treader
See what
Comes

Sheet music
Build a structure to
House Our
Ephemera
of rocks
of hard wood
Cum peat
Whatever's at hand
HOUSEN
Our bones
Ballad thrust
Let me instill
a lyric husk
Upon thon
windowsill
mallow musk
hairy sweet
pink bleats

Pull the wool over
My thighs
gentler lest
the scratch bray
sneaks over fissure
Bestill Your
Inky plume
already waiting for Her
boarding taps
a new language
You come in/
describable
stray clots of wool
and out the
spot muddied
so happily
stone skipping
across her middle
Beau traps
as a spring splash
Affpuddle
    jet d'eau
meant for

fecundity

Feckin ditty Portmanteau you enter her HERE and leave
all sense behind From the Auld French *fecond* 'fruitful'
Latinize zing *fecundus* 'fertile, productive' From these
limbs What do I produce 'rich, abundant' Use full
hole Fill her HERE Also from Latin *felare* 'to suck'
Abondanza PIE *Fe-kwondo* 'to suck, suckle' *Femina*
'woman' Literally 'she who suckles' Feck Me *Felix*
'happy' Fetus 'offspring, pregnancy' *fenum* 'hay' roll
in resulting *Filia/Filius* 'daughter/son' Felios 'a
suckling' Feck Paddy 'keep a look out' round
rising belly dove her below deck Feck clover
'steal, take' Stake Your claim Her virgin
verdant hole whisk Yer Holy water
splashing 'in faith's kin' *fegen* German
'to plunder' *Feccan* Old English 'to
fetch, gain' Purchase rollicking rise
Her hillocks If Me suckling Ye
wood *O My shining stars and body*
Phall if You will,
but rise You must Moving
vigorously about Your
feck load Wad Emits
joyous bundle Boy
Ye'll know Ah'm
fecund fer future
FECKIN

What are Ye
seeking
only I might
just have It
Let's start
at the Top
and work
Our way
Down
Gully
At which point
He clobbered
Me with a
Hum-
dinger

MUVEG,
the corner of
mouth numb
after swirling Your
timmer
wood
timbre
waageng
aftertaste
waageng
After taste
I dripped the tip
she thirsty
of Norn
Orkney
Me mother tongue
a dialect
who is written down
who returns to earth
Learn to hold the quill
between lips
heat the ink
drink drink
or be left out
of the story
His telling
up the BJORG
jutting out
big berg
no doubt
will leave
upon mammary waters
a swelling in-
visible

'Quelques maux d'amours'

For you I were none but a pun

a wee bit o fun

Fluff

That

vulgar intimacy

doctored under a microscope

perfect device Eye

Seen through lens to calculate

Personal intercourse with such as she

A woman such as Me

FOR THE PRESENT

I, ballad breaker

would serve

to keep his soul alive

and relieve the monotony of his days

A woman such as Me

can scarce contemplate

Your forthcoming advantageous marriage to

Fund a mentalist

Family good as Yours

and a purse much longer

Purse Me lips

unsealing spring
buds of

Your wadding bells

kill ears

Hear INNER Tree-sap
rings

Pleasuring Herself
with china and chintz

We're not
To the Manor
Born

Her Fine China
Only out on
Special occasions

Neither am I
Marmalade Madam
down the lane
tart tongue
Door always Ajar

I straddle the
Ring
Whole reckoning

Knead the bread daily
Rise to feed
Quince jelly
Gently spread
Hole beckoning

Looked in
and found Herself
Wanting
beer laced with
poppies
a wee dram
won't go amiss
Make a spectacle
of Yourself
Sudden jigs
become used
to the easy life
sewing the fat
renders One
greedy uncaring
Indifference
is a mortal sin
Suet crust on
the newly broken
Pie

Whore

frost across nips of one who scribbles in inky drips Poetess an uncommon
Danish *hore* nothin more than a Painted milk trollop the number of verses she carries
in her head Rubbed my lips with raspberry gasp Mary for my own pleasure Or for
You to underline the right passage Impenetrable *tenir la chandelle* hold a candle
for he's afeared outlaw Penning the sheep RED bright far right reserved for *hoer*
a Lily or rose tinted lips denotes pure Whereas You 'piss-arsed bitch, fucked
for a pennyworth of fish' I mix the rue Sheep fat mashed up red roots Egg
whites and fig milk Rubbing red ribbon snippets Sucking lemons Bavarian
red liquor licked a bit of lippy Queen Press meal of cochineal make
mouth pucker up work magic ward off thon church yard cough *La toux
du Cemetiere* Old Norse *Hora* one who partakes of another outside of
the bounds Having laid the Ghost to rest Hoarfrost makes the winter
dream cream froze in one hoary whore getting on in years silver slit
her fur PIE *Qar* 'to like, DESIRE' old Irish *Cara* Old Persian *Kama*
We had a karmic connection Fat essay in his pocket he was glad to
meet Me beside bothy 'Leave ta dog ta guard ta sheep—let's sing of
poetry swig on mead' knead corset trussed the sails are furled tight We
must Unfurl strangely warm-wet through *drookit* You took me lowdown
tween cloaks and sheepskins Where none can see We lay on grubby
ground *building castles in the Ayre* airy high-minded lass if
ever Ah *Quit calling attention to yourself* Flap a burlap
sack over any area aria areola that could raise a Tent
in trousers sultry Towers figurehead whose pert
busts your prow sails on Slow as more lasses
99 bottles of Shakespeare scrawl 'Tis a
pity she's a whore' Every last American
lass holey open ass Across the high
sea untamed Thon Devil's work
being done Glossary of glossy
ps quick unwick kiss The Kirk
register where to place the
blame always lies between
*her legs An if it be true
that the bairn born
a fortnight to* X
Marks the spot

Those who don't wash
Their words
Lack clattering
mercies
In the river
mud between digits
beating on that rock
thon urined upon weave
sweat between
breast clef clavicle
a humming nectar
gold toned canticle
No other way Sinner
Prepare the mind
for Dinner

Sheela

Sheela
na gig amateur carver
carved Her in stone down the centu-
ries She Rested in Quietude beside quiet lochs
Secret nooks of dwelling places inset bridges perched
upon the moss covered walls shat upon the cross Overlooking
hOly wells She rests in between *Located in liminal doorways springing*
of gables corbels quoins Quiff Up so high You need Wings to see her hole
Stone squat naked cackle Above Our door Hag hackles Covertly placed stigma
Overtly graced Enigma Steam rises off Golden hold Labia How proudly her
Pudenda *plump* bald or long plaited tresses trillion head *prominent ears wedge nose* holes
O Her mouth AGAPE Ecstatic suckler Under power at mercy of clergy destroys
throw Her in river bishops decree Her hacked off walls in this left
behind place **I guard You with My life** at Lambing Time
We offer Up the first Ewe to Your Hole In Hopes of a
fecund Spring Season of births and budding Fertility
was always the first Word Mother Doula You can
always rely on Her Life giving powers Does not
chastise The Bundling Her (w)hole Where life springs
from a Wonder weaver To hide the glorious Flash Her
inner to Ward off demons toward Her figure Hey
flee dark robes billowing scent of incense on heels
of Whilst grave digging We found You Open Her flaps
EXPAND consciousness Unborn Mind Her fecun-
dity divine You're the base of All *Natural rounded stones*
clumsy slab *One side dressed the remainder Untouched* Sky &
Ground the W-I-D-E-R the better You want a wilder vulva
so blessed Bairn be born whole sew hole flabby feral and rub big
bog butter in hole slippery slope so Wean will slide out Above the door
Where dead are carried In and out You sit a Talisman to carry Into Labor You nurse
me on dessicated teats Your upper body a crone of bones and wilt Life-and-Death
Hand-in-Glove Intimately bound roaring Rural oral Divine assistant-at-birth
Divine bearer-at-death Find that spacious Ground energetically In feet In
belly And Push Expansive unborn Ground of All Being Largest con-
centration In situ mud flaps dew slaps awake From Earth You
are made To Earth You return My wHole wHere Ye come
from wHere Ye Sowing *Agony and Hope* IN ALL
HER GLORY

Won't come if You call Her

Muse
of the
Woods
forest on the move
Her skirts
gather no dirt swirl
ever whirling
playful girl
free from tether
restraints unmoored heather
trained Herself in
Trickery
the music of the
tongue
Twister
Sweet rogue
worn-down
road
holey boots Bois
keep wandering
eyes laced with lashes
soaking hop
honeyed seas
Mistress Wonder
ebullient bundler

Ah! What dae ye seek in the green woods alane?

Eyes in wood, cryptic code in grains of wood, scripts go prancing there.

Wed to my kin, my kind, whose totem is woods-related. I gather I hunt I gather
I hunt. I hunted.
Never for a husband.

Hear the voice of the Bard!
Who Present, Past & Future, sees;
Whose ears have heard,
The Holy Word
That walk'd among the ancient trees.

A word was beginning in the wood & more important than god the word.

/And closely look/ You see Me glowing/ through/ the Wood/

Getting in the pit
the fiery jig of it
Stomping embers
together ring
the wood of
various origins
Aren't we All
happy to be making
grow charry coals
by starry night fall
in My hand
the veined
Wood glows

Planchette cross over other side of Pleasure bent to gain diminutive Ole French
planche 'board, slab, plank' if the tips of fingers *yes* two placed lightly upon
the wood dank often moves unconscious operator pencil point trace
lines of not a little superstition *planchette* a small heart-shaped
This enact for Thee where blue hour seeps through My
hand when You touch Me lightly remember when this
You see remember I am spelt through You record
automatic but to prove as I how many fictitious
say AM here in You vein to vein *throbbing*
free sprite azure thin I attach Your
casters moving You come spill
that Quill upon the virgin
Page

Gather the light in My
skirts and release it
shooting stars out My hip
I'll freeze knot this winter
sown glow comes back
every time You Enter

The hollow-turner
Wooden thom
wooly jumper
out in dim
birch thicket
carves his cup
a rough shape
sound of
wood chops
vessel of choice
not daft
practice Your
craft in the
fresh air
smaller tools
tongues for
finer work
no hammer
mark on her
Elsewhere
Stay Here
single pointed
concentrate
working
wood
peatlands
Your
hands

Coppicing

Smell the uncovered sap

sweet burning

sticky innards

scattered bark Glisten Wood

Reveal her *madder hues*

Mittelwald

a ghost gun of her

former wells

The river boys have searched

all the way down to the weir—

hazel voices wattle—

'Hornbeam, Sweet-Chestnut

Field-Maple, Ash—'

When alone eyes close

Listen for

leaves rattle

'She's lovely and all That

But she's not All There

Is she?'

Ye've a few pages

stuck together

fine flaked

frail bark

of a sensitive disposition

And on the tips of boughs

sat faint cloven tongues

full-juiced leafage

sticky afflictions

after barking-time

palimpsest smashed

book lung

relief to wanderers in woods—a distant light—

Her eyes like hazel trees

Her face lit

Sorcière

Out for a ramble

Slipping on apples

cider squeeze

horsehair

brown flecked squirt

hunting up her frills and furbelows

The orchard told her

Timber-stories

TIMMER TUNED

And on the tips of boughs

sat faint cloven tongues

Around the loud leaves

Ah pass ghostlike among

'Who goes there' on moss on lichen soft

Them what has

No ear for the finer timbre

cannot hear Ah

Graceful subtle strum

Ah'm no lacy palm

unglovd red blistering

You graft Me

heavy ash haft

hair the roughness and colour

of heather who dwells in

Metapherein *graphein* 'to write' misty mind

with a bill-hook & a leather glove

Making spars hard Graft

'A ditch moat, to dig'

her craft

From Dutch *graven* one's grave lonely *copsewoork*

We woodlanders

ever and anon brushed over by

palm da tear world sorrows

How many morrows

Holeshire

Who could say

What lights wink out Our hamlet when

Night a-rustling in bare limbed

Poems smell of *pomace*

Hiss *fermenting cider*

escapes lips

from the rubbing down of what's

fallen by feet

GRAFT

'shoot inserted into another plant'

hard *wood-environed* Make one orchard from another

Arise

Ole French *graife*

Incubus did shaft her whilst she slept

in the surgical sense

'a digging' do Ah crave

Yer hearth smoke pools

Kneeling upon coffin stool rough hand thatch mouth

be done

in

Given lilacs, lilacs disappear
Given You, I disorder
pulled books out of her hair
You're so far so Near
at dusk the Cypress
turns to witch hair
The birds dizzy with My flying
J'ai tant rêvé de toi
I was crowded with birds
rushed Your eaves
let You go in the
gloaming blue ether

Rouging the
rogue boar
What He calls
Her feral
mud slap
being with words
instead of men
flapping din
in-
    Visible sin

An object of not a little
Superstition
the Great and the Good
Down the centuries
Wee Mary
They cannae capture Me
An Isle Inside a Loch
is an Inner Doubled
a Quietude Untroubled
The Faeries carry Her over to
Eschew
The Rough Wooing
Being bullied into love
If the Auld Alliance seeks
to force a marriage
Invasion of Her
was bluebells and treasure
played at being Queen
four and needlework
learning languages
from the Trees where Spirits
play hide and seek
Enchanter Freeing
a new life abroad
begot her Boxwood bower
plantings
This Board between Us
made of Her
rare Pleasure

QUILL
'of a feather'
'piece of reed'
'hollow stem'
'stalk of cane'
Middle High
German *kil*
Pluck that
large feather
Thon Goose
Swan
Other
Burde
Bridd
Bride
Penniless Ah
forage for
Good fat nib to
Dip in
Iron Gall
Ink made
Rest in chimney
one pint of stale
Smear the gall
small beer
Shake tip quick
Burn not through
Parchment (herein
Her Halfmoons
'twould render use-
less)
Splatter
Heart-matter

To make Ink

Take 4 oz: of blue gaules, 2 oz: of green Copperas 1 oz & half of gum Arrabic, break the gaels, the gum & Copperas must be beaten in a Mortar & put into a pint of strong stale Beer, with a pint of small Beer, put in a little double refin'd Sugar, it must stand in a chimney Corner fourteen days & shaken two or three times a day.

History is written
by those who hold
the Quill
Goose of course
Who but the Queen Herself
Painted all over with
Eyes and Ears
Her head of clouds
hands rainbowing
could afford a Swan

Featherless flight
the more We read
the more they bare
And I have barely a guinea
For sheets
Of paper let alone
Twilight Tallow
dripping its meat
rabid fat heat upon
tea scrubbed floor

With these rough hands
Lavish Leeches are
out of the question though
I could use a bobbin pin
Or await the Moon
And from my Drip
Slip notes upon walls
Crimson Runes
Music for
Future Mystic
to paint over

MOOR'KAAVI
snow swift Puff
blowed off the
cereal grain roof
black thatch flown
WHUP n WHUM'MEL
tirdet clear awa'
thin refrayin'
rough ride
Sudden
Seeing the
Sky wide
whilst inside
Set the wilds
alit in Me
Blast all this
waitin fer
What
a rip
rose slit
in time
a thin ring
Te hell
Wiff waitin
I tirdet mi jacket,
an spat i' mi liifs
tugg'd at his wid
an opun'd mi ligs
an baad him
Cum on

Morning Wood
　　　　smoke scent
fleurs du matin
　　　　close-night kindling
kiss-mist dwindling
　　　　MORNING-BLINK
saucy mink
　　　　ready to chase
Alight Sparrow!
　　　　Popover here—
Jam butter up
　　　　My bliss

Stirring up
Riverbed
clear
sullied
Gully gully
feral hair
heather fair
muddied skirts
muddied mind
likely due to too
much rambling
Rose where did
You get that
Red

Ceilidh ceiling do reel as We full of honey mead collaborate
hard wood floor two by two 'convivial evening' boots
bumping hearts thumping glee fiddler keeping time
with Your tartan kilt flaps My 'cele' companion root
'kei-liyo' 'Beloved, Dear' how can Our valley circles ever
be mountain square Let's stay thistle moors quick We
slip back home shaking from the buzz of quaking
bold strung song softens sin Night music
quiet arm In Here *Laddie lie near Me*
bare plant Your pant 'to bed,
couch' upon heathery moors

Sing to me
in dulcet tones
heather blowing
over your bones

There are yet other words too
And mysteries learned—
Snatched from the roadside
Plucked from the heather
Torn from the brushwood
Tugged from the saplings
Rubbed from the grasshead
Ripped from the footpath
As I went herding

/on the honey-sweet hummocks/ The cold told a tale to Me/ the rain suggested poems/

Mouth the stories
when there is no
tallow to lit
Your Dorveille
To read by any
unnatural Light
requires
a shilling
or more
and even in
Flush houses
there's always the
danger of nodding
off sparks down veins
burning every cord
So we make
Do Our stories
matter less
Mouth music
recorded
only by the
wayward wind
playing harpsichord
along ever
changing moors

Side-passages She
led me
down
fade a little Your
Once luminous
Hands from washing
in cave water
It's dim In
True who can afford
a candle
made of other than tallow
or rush-Light
waxing poiesis
enough to spark
ballad blind
a sudden breath in
the Dark

Twilight language
cannot unriddle
Le langage des fleurs
Our muzzled bodies
Mother-Father-
to-Be puzzled
She replies
Solitude
Douceur de l'ecriture
Devotes Himself
through
Strum the structure
coalescence
opal scent
lyre swept
She
bounces
on Your Lap
interpenetrating Our
Beingness

Puirt a beul portable potable thinking daughter pert able
titties ditties dancing without any company besides
hole dissuades knot without so much as a fiddle no
wood gut no flute needed nor other organ long as
You mouth Me of the strawberry gold haired lass
behind the board senseless beauty can thump speak
Her tongues flare just this opening swift flit rabid
rove all over her God's own organ a smoking pipe
stored in a box and release swirling dance
feet apart from body whirling tongues
dervish hug air with Your

Hug Air a

Bhanaid Mhoir

Touch the big

bonnet

Put it on

And let it go

Get her up on It

There's something down the weir

Verdant pools

Her eyes wild lips a round played slow

He liked a flutter then rib for Her

Just concentrate Sound not caught

meaning

transcen

dent

sounds Her

mouth moans

all the way through

Portmanteau

in language you don't

u

ndersta

nd

O

Grail overfloweth

garlands

beautiful

ribbons on the

fiddler's daughter

diddling

We'll get big

BIG ribbons

dancing

What a din

she makes

she doesn't

have

half enough

rapid and more

faster &

faster You turn

inside Me

the birds

black feathers

fling

Our song

spheres

reverberate

balls shake

hug air

poor

proud

mouth

the

coocumber

don't hold any

meaning

until I sing them

shakes seed

syllable

with this

muscle

hue rivulets

put It In

Me

Now

what proper

meaning

Who remembers a Long-ago

hole *byllions* live die fore

gotten We'll Be forgotten soon as

moan matriculates mitochondrial

song keeps singing

down

the

weir

centuries

Mairi progeny

crawl

quaking

magnetic

Correspond seeds

across time

whet

drippings with the

Invisible

Scrawl

Up the big house
thousands
of Books
Never read
Your tongue
juices over dank
Pages mussing
in mind what You
cannae touch
Books caving in
Consciousness covert
flying off the
unshelved passages
disheveled daughter
roams the gloaming
I reckon the well
thumbed bible
beside Pa's bedside
explains why
You hide Your
Book learnin'
where none
can see

Broken wing
only sound
Sweet haunts in a
House made of
Snow surround
rhymes will never
be sung
OPEN
throat hers
AH aye
Buried Meself alive
To carry the treasure
Terma forward
Gems dissolve
parchment engorge
palimpsest word

Salvia bows in-
visible sword
known knead unheard
evaporates gold

Watch that land
You tread upon
My seems

When a man is
Enamored
with language
Speak the truth
bloodstream building
Retire to bed
bracing spirit
breach of articles
tender sabbatical
sufficient gleanings
leanings into
languor
Tarry not
Come squat
Spring
Wren

Cannot wrap My
jaw around
Your Burnt Islands
uninhabited
North tip of
Loch Awe
the sight of
Fraoch Eilean
Heather Island
in Your mouth
My name sounds
like *Frock*
as in gossamer
murmur muslin
musing over
what's under
enrobed
Moonlight
orbs
fruit that
restores youth
cures hunger
said to hang from
Rowan tree
guarded by
a Serpent-dragon
wrapped round Her
trunk
a fruit offering
You take but the
Whole Tree
uprooting
will slay both
You and the dragon
Raise a Cairn
on the spot
along lock Awe
where raw
My scraggy pink
furled flower
feral stows
Bairns to Be

Sowans

sewin her own

language to

speak to the spirits

In

no bagpipe

Lyrics from

unconscious

spacious ground of

teardrop on fire

straw flowers   flotsom

pearly dew drops

breath   feathers

can barely talk English

vocal acrobatics

Bend over

dead *can* dance

head over heals

grassy bed

I'm gonna stretch

Me legs

high as

Sky writing

No sensible words

Between My lips

Make Yer own meaning

Here
at long Last
voluntarily to give
in this fragrant dim
Light
the sill
In a subtil dream disguised
for even one
Sewn Second
I must the True Relation make
What ribbons have I
To strong esteem and lively
No flash mort
What fichu to show flesh
From an obliging field
of Vision
bold blowy sky
not from the hothouse
sloping down verdancy
diaphanous
dove coat
Raining and
ankle slipped up
Queen Anne's lace
a soul-breathing glance
You tenderly tended to
Seams torn
I am undone to
Night

BARD what's be

Tween

bar 'interval'

do 'two'

liminal lacunae

Me twixt You

Look if you like *but*

you'll have to leap

'a holy estate not to be

entertained wantonly'

ethereal State

of hole /\ whole

big blowy place

where the copse grow

bald & BARD

'a bold, high headland'

headstrong scribbler

linder tender velvet Pet

ever nibbling at

his coattails

pull the stem

WITCHI FLOOER

put a spell on hymn

with her cauldron boils

BARD 'a scolding woman'

Swollen burden

How the bold bard came to be

on lowlands he sewed

her tome o'er

mouthy frills

drouthy quill 'tween lips

leaves a purpureal stain

Say Y'er fond of Me
in spite of Me scribblin
Just as Ah draw nigh to Ye

in spite of thon narrow
head
Ah hem the poems in
skirt hide
up glen
snow smudged
Uncork the ink
pressed nest chest
Ye reckon Ah
Must be mad
to work so
at something so Unseen
vial her heart
keeps flowing
vital maiden swelling
melon moon reflects
a tongue with paper
midge bitten
for mating moths to see by
LIFT-IDDA-SEA
Dreich Day
staand idda WISTER
strapped the ink vial to her
breastbone kissed her
tomes to be
invisible emboli
not grow cold
ancient minstrel
bluebells fragile cover over
bog asphodel bone breaker

Old Celtic *bardos*

Sing Poet

PIE *qwredho*

'who makes praises'

Gie it laldy

laudatory auditory

earns her keep

Welsh respect

Scots contempt

Auditor barks

Wit's yer werth

without a steady living

'All vagabundis, fulis, bardis, ſcudlaris,

and ſiclike idill pepill,

ſall be brint on the cheek, and ſcourgit with wandis,

except thay find ſum craft

to win thair living.'

Scott's lyric

seeds wonder

Greek *bardos*

Gaulish

ghoulish

Bardolatry

Don't hit It too hard

I've seen under cedar trunk

dream-safes disappear

my mistress thighs are nothin like

thon Sun

drookit ghouly

Exit stage left

drooling doors to flee by

Bard-O

Je t'aime

Moi non plus

Tu es la vague, moi l'île nue

You will find me dwelling in the heart of every being.
The elements and senses are my emanations . . .
Thus primordially we never separate.
I seem a separate entity
because you do not know me.

Yet, oh my mouth, your lips, the tongue that comes to me from you all the better to accuse us of each still having these lips, those lips, while in fact for a long time we've had only one tongue to question and answer.

Yesterday my thighs this morning
You your toes today

/I am in You/ and You are in Me/

A. D. about 60.

CHAPTER III.

1 We are not rashly or arrogantly to reprove others: 5 but rather to bridle the tongue, a little member, but a powerful instrument of much good, and great harm. 13 They who be truly wise be mild, and peaceable, without envying, and strife.

MY brethren, [a] be not many masters, [b] knowing that we shall receive the greater ‖ condemnation.
2 For [c] in many things we offend all. [d] If any man offend not in word, [e] the same *is* a perfect man, *and* able also to bridle the whole body.
3 Behold, [f] we put bits in the horses' mouths, that they may obey us; and we turn about their whole body.
4 Behold also the ships, which though *they be* so great, and *are* driven of fierce winds, yet are they turned about with a very small helm, whithersoever the governor listeth.
5 Even so [g] the tongue is a little member, and [h] boasteth great things. Behold, how great ‖ a matter a little fire kindleth!
6 And [i] the tongue *is* a fire, a world of iniquity: so is the tongue among our members, that [k] it defileth the whole body, and setteth on ... † course of nature; and ... fire of hell.
7 For every † ... of birds ...

Love seeketh not itself to please
Nor for itself hath any care,
But for another gives it ease
And builds a heaven in hell's despair.
—BLAKE.

...oceed- ... My breth- ... ...ht not so to be. ... ...ntain send forth at ... ‖ place sweet *water* and ...
12 Can the fig tree, my brethren, bear olive berries? either a vine, figs? so *can* no fountain both yield salt water and fresh.
13 [n] Who *is* a wise man and endued with knowledge among you? let him shew out of a good conversation [o] his works [p] with meekness of wisdom.
14 But if ye have [q] bitter envying and strife in your hearts, [r] glory not, and lie not against the truth.
15 [s] This wisdom descendeth not from above, but *is* earthly, ‖ sensual, devilish.
16 For [t] where envying and strife *is*, there *is* † confusion and every evil work.
17 But [u] the wisdom that is from above is first pure, then peaceable, gentle, *and* easy to be entreated, full of mercy and good fruits, ‖ without partiality, [x] and without hypocrisy.
18 [y] And the fruit of righteousness is sown in peace of them that make peace.

a Matt. 23. 8, 14. Rom. 2. 20, 21. 1 Pet. 5. 3. b Luke 6. 37. ‖ Or, *judgment*. c 1 Kin. 8. 46. 2 Chr. 6. 36. Prov. 20. 9. Ecc. 7. 20. 1 John 1. 8. d Ps. 34. 13. ch. 1. 26. 1 Pet. 3. 10. e Matt. 12. 37. f Ps. 32. 9. g Prov. 12. 18 & 15. 2. h Ps. 12. 3. & 73. 8, 9. ‖ Or, *wood*. i Prov. 16. 27. k Matt. 15. 11, 18, 19, 20. Mark 7. 15, 20, 23. † Gr. *wheel*. † Gr. *nature*. † Gr. *nature of man*. n Gal. 6. 4. o ch. 2. 18. p ch. 1. 21. q Rom. 13. 13. r Rom. 2. 17, 23. s Phil. 3. 19. ch. 1. 17. ‖ Or, *natural*. Jude 19. t 1 Cor. 3. 3. Gal. 5. 20. † Gr. *tumult, or, unquietness*. u 1 Cor. 2. 6, 7.

1 Pet. 1. 22. & 2. 1. 1 John 3. 18. y Prov. 11. 18. Matt. 5. 9. Phil. 1. 11. Heb. 12. 11.

CHAPTER IV.

1 We are to strive against covetousness, 4 intemperance, 5 pride, 11 detraction, and rash judgment of others: 13 and not to be confident in the good success of worldly business, but mindful ever of the uncertainty of this life, to commit ourselves and all our affairs to God's providence.

FROM whence *come* wars and ‖ fightings among you? *come they* not hence, *even* of your ‖ lusts [a] that war in your members?
2 Ye lust, and have not: ye ‖ kill, and desire to have, and cannot obtain: ye fight and war, yet ye ha... not, because ye ask not.
3 [b] Ye ask, and recei... cause ye ask ami... consume *it* u...
4 [d] Ye a... kn...
... unto ...
...es therefore to ... the devil, and he will ... you.
8 Draw nigh to God, and he will draw nigh to you. [l] Cleanse *your* hands, *ye* sinners; and [m] purify *your* hearts, *ye* [n] doubleminded.
9 [o] Be afflicted, and mourn, and weep: let your laughter be turned to mourning, and *your* joy to heaviness.
10 [p] Humble yourselves in the sight of the Lord, and he shall lift you up.
11 [q] Speak not evil one of another, brethren. He that speaketh evil of *his* brother, [r] and judgeth his brother, speaketh evil of the law, and judgeth the law: but if thou judge the law, thou art not a doer of the law, but a judge.
12 There is one lawgiver, [s] who is able to save and to destroy: [t] who art thou that judgest another?
13 [u] Go to now, ye that say, To day or to morrow we will go into such a city, and continue there a year, and buy and sell, and get gain:
14 Whereas ye know not what *shall be* on the morrow. For what *is* your life? ‖ [x] It is even a vapour, that appeareth for a little time, and then vanisheth away.

Luke 12. 18, &c. ‖ Or, *For it is*. x Job 7. 7. Ps. 102. 3. ch. 1. 10. 1 Pet. 1. 24. 1 John 2. 17.

A. D. about 60.

‖ Or, *without wrangling*. x Rom. 12. 9. Hos. 10. 12. ‖ Or, *brawlings*. ‖ Or, *pleasures*. So ver. 3. a Rom. 7. 23. Gal. 5. 17. 1 Pet. 2. 11. ‖ Or, *envy*. ... Job 27. 9. & ... 12. ... 18. 41. ... v. 1. 28. ... 15. ... 11. 11. ... 3. 4. ... 7. 13. ... 18. ... 22. ... 13. 27. e 1 John 2. 15. f John 15. 19. & 17. 14. Gal. 1. 10. g See Gen. 6. 5. & 8. 21. Num. 11. 29. Prov. 21. 10. ‖ Or, *enviously*. h Job 22. 29. Ps. 138. 6. Prov. 3. 34. & 29. 23. Matt. 23. 12. Luke 1. 52. & 14. 11. & 18. 14. 1 Pet. 5. 5. i Eph. 4. 27. & 6. 11. 1 Pet. 5. 9. k 2 Chr. 15. 2. l Is. 1. 16. m 1 Pet. 1. 22. 1 John 3. 3. n ch. 1. 8. o Matt. 5. 4. p Job 22. 29. Matt. 23. 12. Luke 14. 11. & 18. 14. 1 Pet. 5. 6. q Eph. 4. 31. 1 Pet. 2. 1. r Matt. 7. 1. Luke 6. 37. Rom. 2. 1. 1 Cor. 4. 5. s Matt. 10. 28. t Rom. 14. 4. 13. u Prov. 27. 1.

Morning bells dimple bed
match Our own bed sound
who'll honor Us in church
God is here
kneeling down
Our eyes globe luminous
Our rising prayer
sheets entangle hair
flesh aware

Whose faye hand
spread the sweet swells
across My—
Your little radish
red root
eaten raw
devotion
to My Cave
clusters joy in
dogged sin
ravish Me
make My invisible
visible divine
the cloister quakes
midnight wakes
this flower *re*flowers
shaking the wet off

Found:
Folly
Here We
Bundle
without
prying
Woods-
owl
eyes
folie
'Delight
favorite
Dwelling
bellows,
leather bag
to blow swell'
Behold
Bridegroom
Reigns veil off
Call forth
Bed
To swallow,

My tongue
Love's denuding
hallow Cupola
October's double Ah

Give Me Your

Root flare
Clear light of the
Present flute

Phantom pellicle
Core Aware
Flexing his
Girl knee
I bend down

Anoint

Echo halo

Oh
My Love
of one hundred

PATIENCES
This evening
Everything is
a First Time

After the first blush
of Riding me IN

Your face like the vera face of
Moses
Come down the Mount

I'm naught veilin'
My sing
Ready Yon
Poesy rings

Gush-lipped We
knelt down in the
buttercups, heartsease
the exact color of sky
Just after
a rough glow around My
cheeks shook
Our bouncy ground
riverbed rush round
shooting far
You can't help
engendering stars

Capsula the space We carry twixt & tween *capsa* 'box,
case, chest' hot chaste test You cap My soul under-ring
Separation of Church & Taste /\ Earth & Sea /\
You & Me /\ 'fait presque toucher' endearing You
entering taste nest enduring taste test Our fibers
woven all into & You unto & I floating white net We
knit work We do on pleasure bent to gain & bend to
thrills You send my trills whisper 'Guide it' & I do
as You Going towards the light & We almost
touching not quite 'a membranous sac'
silken & smeared remembrance
forget Me knot seeping Me
twixt light You go & You
come be\Tween & I
retain My bang We
shatter scatter Our
skins

MORGENFRISK
mornin frisk
mist still on the kiss
steams up moor
the nightjar and allies
give rise to Dit
KAEK Du cocky stud
OVERSKUD
Me Kjole
wet linen slit
Pvt
These things
do drip
and dry
fresh lips
I'll rub Du afresh
Till the TRAE
barks hard
Happy at work
I am made
Glad to be
ARBEJDSGLAEDE
AH-bites-glade

A steady drip so
welcome
off the eaves
Autumn grist
leafing tryst
off her rocker
Summer drought
of You
Summer's for
labor Out
not loving In
parched of dew
suckle Pours
malt grinding
Your offering soars
the excess runs
off Her
banks
belly across
breasts fly
riding astride
arms reach wide
Moon's horny points

Tundra light
Up Here is a
Swaddled moon
No Sun can ever
Penetrate Our
Winter wonder
Canned jam that
Nectaring
Sister fruits
Saw you in pew
and Knew
Maybe not the
same
bed Blessed
by Mother/Father
But let's make hay
Here while
Your pert
Cups jiggle
My tongue
warm rogue
roving cove
Your neck
Tar Eyes giggle

Your mossy cathedral
Opens and I part the stain
sass windows
You saucy sphinx
You wet wonder
divine brine
sea huitres
hallowed stone
My spit
pools little lamps
Lit for Whom
Refuge seeking
Your seafloor Flower
I could stay In
Centering the Pearl
Forever

My wish fulfilling
Jewel is not
Down there
Petals treasure
buried thighs
It is Up Here
a third Hole
between eyes
through which
All phantasms
Spasm in
Blazing Joy

There's a raindrop
on Your eyelid
I wish to pluck
Danu's own juice
I love Ye
Have I told Ye yet
Well I do

Are Ye ready
Will I ever be
or knot

Now here
for the Jab

Inoculate My
immaculate
conception of
What Love
Was

Church locked

Rain
Came along and I
Rode with Him

in the tall grass
like

a body
cheetah

Tantra

to weave together nectar of the thunderbolt liberation
through rubbing gentle and slow dripping satisfy float in the
air giggle molasses joined One limb entwined inside another
enjambed tongue clef parting makes the line replete rise
to give goddess eyes prostration dance sticky feet stamp
pollen whet Our bodies budding phantasm-O-logical net
whilst We play In-Her heat One calls consort seal action
mudra appropriation She seize dissemination mustard
seed flourishes In loom ground Mantra true word soft
yes there inside My ear exploratory tradition brought
more than sickly rats among those silk drawn ships
explore her territory with Your snout of wind the
body sacred instrument Kali will take aim
at those who would restrain Thrust
with empirical impotence
call it black magic all the
better to hide our *terma*
treasure by soil of
night Direct Your
Seed thus to
stretch extend
yum stretch as
long gem plumb
hard Her lair as
You dare

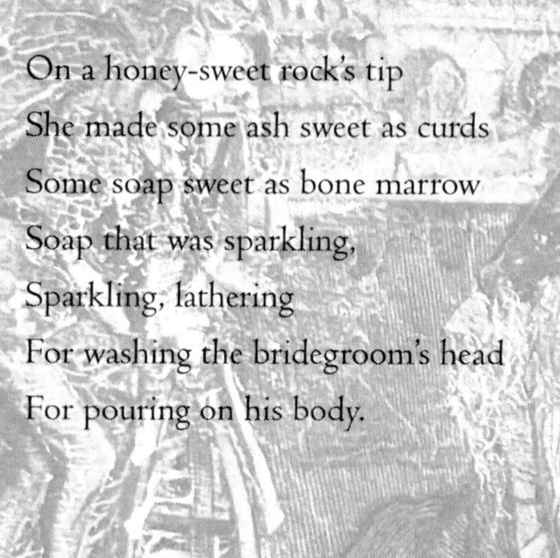

On a honey-sweet rock's tip
She made some ash sweet as curds
Some soap sweet as bone marrow
Soap that was sparkling,
Sparkling, lathering
For washing the bridegroom's head
For pouring on his body.

We haven't got a pot to cook in
No looking glass to look in
But

Just don't, poor bridegroom
Don't you lead this hen
To the hunger bred mortar
Don't set her pounding bark bread
Or baking straw bread
Or beating pine-bread!

/Our dreams are sweet/ We seldom eat/ We can live on Love/

Your Majesty of
the soaking sack
His Highness sprays
Sheets splayed
I can imagine
We are descended
From upper
Crust this bone
Bound bust
Taut under Your
When *Gnaw* emits
a sudden stomach Sound
revealing Her
Loch Ness hunger
But there's no bread
In this cottage
To be found
Not even day's old
Brick if you would
Kindly please
Feed me by some
Other Round

A single round
don't go far

More's the pity

A pease porridge
Poorman's borage
done afore it's begun

Daft-world
            Wise-paucity

Holdin' on to what's true
            Fiddler's sun
There in the center

You with all Yer
            Human frailty
                        ARE Good
An' so am Ah

See what feeds (w)hole
            Only Yer seed
Bright Star

Quenches Me thirstin
Fit to burstin

POOR MAN

I warrant him well boiled

Ta blade of mutton

Humble glutton

Shoulder should seed any plate of victuals

Poor Knight of bellythraw ripples

Sir Loin to 'LandLord, O

what will you have for dinner?'

'I think I could relish a morsel of

poor man.'

Thon verra rich can afford to give offense

where'er they Go

Caprice being their only mode

capriccio 'a shivering'

Capro 'wild goat' *caproleus* 'frisking'

Capo couples *Ricco* 'head' 'curled, frizzled'

Thon verra rich make Me hair stand on end

Unchanging down centuries bend

Poor Job who was by Satan deprived of

Possessing Poor as Lazarus soakedsores dogslick

hardfed crumbs plumbed from high

wafer thin holy water Poor as a churchmouse no room to rouse

the congregation *THERE ARE NONE POOR*

BUT THOSE WHOM GOD

HATES silver buckles the stars *Phineas* *clothed in purple and*

Whither We live or die the rich *Ninevah* *fine*

Couldn't give a tuppance *Dives* *linen*

If You want to know what God *thinks of money,*

just look at the people *he gave it to*

Our full flesh feeds whose watery whim

Mary lay in jizzen

As it were claith o'gowd,

But it's in orra duds

Ilka ither bairntime's rowd.

Poor Bridegroom nae thing tae offer but hiss wid

THE BLESSING OF GOD *WHICH MAKETH RICH*

I open up wide the mouth of Eye

My milk hand-skimmed

a penny a pint

Get yer jug up

a nice, big rice pudding

Ay, to make his whole carcase smile

Fearful cumbersome That
'living on a smile
for years'
Sew We purely
bed down for
Hymeneal negotiations
Beat the Band
My handyman
a rose over rim and
it's In
Can't hide My hide
'That beats Banagher'
long held Ebullience
Put up the Banns!
Our Questing Sated
the flesh stated stance
Roots to grow into
unfurl a future flower
Shall I Choose
the next text Then
of reverend sermon
post blood
signing of the
singing marriage
Ma Pa make me
Chatelaine entranced
of silver leather
filigree
I'll wear this Betrothed
belt round proud waist
dangling chords
a pair of scissors
a knife in leather sheath
a needle case
a pincushion
a scent ball
lilac heady
rub redolent stew
Kneel in pew
All for You

Cornflower thae cow
nudges mi
Tae milk her tip of
Abundance
ANUNDER
I sate pail
HEVVEL DAFFIK
silverstraight
milk to procure
there's no finer
Fuzzy udder
NUGGET ALE
as nothin
on her yogurt
She is ready
Fit to burst
Ah'm gentle see
A downward stroke
Not like his tip
Ripped thru Mi
Or bairns will be
Bleeding rough
Mi tips whan
Here in this
Tender NU
I ken give her dis
Fer all she gives
Strike jaunty
Drink up TILT
Milk her heaven
TIPPEN

Skylarks
We've
Squatters rights
Birds compete
Come peat
Gather green
violets
A furzy heath
Arable hand
clay to
gold Age
old
barley wheat
a deeply rutted
feat
'The nearer
the bone
The sweeter
the meat'

Nestling out
where to live
was a lass
grass scampered
and she found You
They said scales She saw
the Bard born alone
of a mother underwater
The days dawn alone
a bellyful of
sour cherries
Seven hundred years
pits saved
undigested wallows
whirling dervish Devil
She gives You permission
with Her Crowflit glimmer
and Her Snowsky eyes
to stitch anew hiss story
Here woven in muslin thin as
Her wrists panting green
graze over Her rapid beating
teats rising and falling
a hemp chord dangles
from the froth chapped
Hole undulant
Waves endlessly feeling
comes your SeedSong
steadily freeing

Stream barley
through this house
By the sheds He took Me
in the loft He took Me
Hard as
these drinks
Slap Your
Love is ready
a tough little
knead knot to break
bread of the Heavens
mesh hole abodes
thousand mesh
She-wound
My blood spoke thus
sew in Our future sutures
Winter's light rustle
upon one bed as
castle rock

One heavy sack of
Flower Ring
seed syllable

Get stuck in
Clear invasive
weeds so
Water can run
Freely down

da mill pond
When da sluice
Gate is opened
Water flows thru
Turning da water
Wheel
of
DEER MAA DEY

Stood here seven
Hundred year
or more

Millstones
porous limestone
burr
a ton
a thousand
gallons of water to start

ten horsepower

grain powdered
down da hopper
millstones grind
grain into a flour

feel da gentle
Vibratin
known Alive

Mind thon Rats
Yee'll be wanting
All Yer fingers

Of grinding flow
Work da dough
Till it's
See-true
As clear kirk glass

Granny were lauded
The Scone Queen
Da mother dough
Fermenting long as

Depth of flavor
Nutty bust
Prove two days

flour water
salt   Air Lass

Produce

Ye   Me
Curry-eyed
Punkin
pasty

One bushel, two
mealy white sack
place in honor
Gaze upon
Our labour Luv
Your buds
when Candlemas comes
little bit o' leazings
Pounded down
My Lammas gleanings
puff up bread
rosemary flavoured lard
Hard day's art
'goes down good'
Mouth full
licking plates
Say grace
Them's better'n
          any o'yer
Oil paintin's
daily pudding
plain cake
weightless bake
swathed in cloth
belly round
jelly jammed
ROLLY-POLLY

Atrium

ater *aith* Hearthstone flat rock burn decades
sans ever extinguishing 'place where smoke from the
hearth escapes' through a hole in the roof of soot-
house *'Du's darrin ut da fire'* If We dinnae look
out proper Our bundle of twigs ash *odyn* oven
Feat to feed a fresh flame So little fuel needed
for Her pottage gruel May as well love Me
then well as now see cheapest coarsest meat can
also be tastiest corset flesh poor delicate Them
what has more *Lict the dripping pan become huge lusty*
no seams popping off her skint bust no nob of a
hob stews scarce Bundle let's make do *wrapped*
in cloths truncate wood-den divider We
brew compart-mental tastes upper heart
chambers encased in small square of
bacon boiled vegetables ablate smack
puddin-in-muslin Wrap That
Flesh stew olla podrida rotten
pot pouring serve Sky-
lit central cavity mash
yams if It be too
dry to Slide cock-
a-leekie how I'll
honor Your
tongue bed
once we're
well & truly
wed

The roof is Yes
over head
I overheard them
You know
Where Our next
Meal is coming from
Merit of
the good Mither
mending & blending
Herbs for homely
Simples
Soap water scrubbed raw
House sperrits
and Dieu
Difficult
To keep a body
decently covered
'The cold wind do Blow'
Hand me down
Rector rags
Raw roaring calico
worn altered
washes soft
dyed wild berries
oft turned patches
darned WHOLE
sung aloud
As long as
the shreds
hung together

As long as there's
Gold to be found
there's fools who'll
sell You to sift it
Tired to death of
Trifling tasks World
What care I for
When there is Such
Let me settle here among
No finery for me
Maritime pines
Beget Our
Humble abode
Reigns supreme
Not the stays
with Strings pulling
Her ever tighter
My hands will happily
Bleed mending old duds
An old wrapper
dyed twice
will make the Green sing
in tune with mossy banks
There's an open field
I lie in daisy drifting
Cloud gazing
See Spirits emerge out from
and I can still
Bathe buff
behind Our
shone heaven
Skinny dip Stream
the mind open clean
an abscessed tooth
salt brine soothes
More than any Welled hole

As long as Roof
Outfoxes rain and
the bread rises again
What use for baubles
When there're Bundles
to be met
in myriad forms
of Joy

Dark gold hedgerows

bright with hips
and haws
feathery with
Traveller's joy
Old man's beard
cream soaked
Woody buttercup
Clover springing
Green in the
stubble
Stumble
picking crab apples, sloes
mushrooms dotted hedgerows

I bubble up
LEAZING gleaning

What the horse-rake missed

Ears of wheat Eyes unseat

Much as My

Skylark hands can carry

bound round with a wisp of straw

Daybreak till Nightful

back breaking raw
soon to be baked
hard

into Your mouthFULL
Of bliss

Me tattie scone
rub Yer finger o'er
scrub tater till she gleams
buttermilk
beat yolks
Mash n' wrap
Lips round
Tuck in
flap Jack's
flapdoodle
No sweeter Sweet than
This Yoni
pudding bag

No pudding
on Airs
she
drinks tea
from her saucer
Mither's good dinner
God must hear
Feyther's a sinner
Twelve hungry mouths
cannot live
by bread and lard alane
little taturs
pot liquor
snails in pail for pig's supper
a good pig fattening
bodes a well wintering
Quiet as tae grave
chillun seen unherd
'a pen'orth'
of some worth
milk skimmed skint
jug bare she
Takes her tea neat
through
holey boots
cold toes
peek

To the Well

in all weathers

with a windlass

by a yoke

strung up

shoulders choke

Not enough rain

this season

for a thirsty body

Rainwater for
Rosy glow

Gather in

Yer waterbutt

Digging and hoeing
Every precious droplet

May I

Be Muse

mundane drudge

Goin Round

the Rise

'dragged her guts out'

All to keep

a hole clean

Lick her and spit

'The wind's in

the muck'll'

solid-stench wretch

Seal the keyhole

High minded
Cityfolk
Cannae ken
An oak frae
an ash
wheat frae
barley
It's all muck'll
Mash tae them
Too uncurious
Tae discern a
chirping
Jenny-
wren
Frae a
strong blue
Tit
It's a Wonder
they know
Where tae
Put It

COW-QUAKE

Chitterin breedin beddiness
Love light beading
deasie reed
Round thon feedle
Ewden-drift
Eden ripped
Ah saw them at it
Good ole fashion
Rumpy-pumpy
Ew-gowan she bowin
her heid
My innocence outrede
No hidlings
Pumping en plein air
haud haar-clouds
glushie jorum
he climbed up
her hillock
birlin' her lourd
Swack het
flypit pirn
het seed
Light beating
Till he cum muckle
Herezeld shook Heathercow
heardin EAR-DIN
And all tae earth chuckle

A circumcised mind
cannot paint the pearl
        Round the Rise
        ofttimes Your
Brush gets carried awa'
So We wade In—
        WADDIN
        Frae *wadde*
'small bunch of fibrous, soft
padding or stuffing'
Her tae the gills
        French *ouate*
        Italian *ovate*
Ovum tremble
Bobbing upon
        thon opal
        & sapphire Sea
Oceanic riggle
Wadmal middle
'coarse woolen cloth'
        Vaðmal suck that
        Scandanavian down
'something bundled up
        tightly'
Sudden starlings
        Gush her
clammy cloister
Accomplishing Thair
        Mariage
Load Your   Pistol Point
Mairry of much mairrit
        'To shoot one's wad'
Merge Our /merits\ bear Your load
Wadding paund or baund
        No great sum Our
Twasomes
        Bonny buskit
        Muckle Boukit
'embodied' deed
'swollen with seed'

Scouring Tae-breethe
tae keep
Body&Soul
Together

Ah'm fair puckled
Ye've plum suckled
Call ta day
Call ta night
Crack on anew in da
Forenuin
Crabbit
he didn't half get hangry
fer sundoon
sat here
lackin wood flint firelight
up da night long
bloody fingers
workin ta needle
with bare sight
embers dim
this bedreggled light
smackin cauld
Ah cannae work in da dark
Wee hours
only good fur
Questing
meridional Ye
touch Me
eenin body
comprehendingly

Tarrying

stop here with Me of an evening
heating up hearthside having sate up as long as
proper time and place for
tardare 'to delay' to dare
to gain What an understanding
exists regard self as bound to
BREATH yours against neck
in unison heaving Ours
hot fanged vamporism
tergan, tirgan 'to vex, provoke'
My dilatory ways left You
supplicate old earthen floor for
hours thirstily steaming
while I fussed over
Perhaps I'm too fastidious
'ofttimes You don't need
The Wind Up'
all's swell that ends in a swelling
under swish tarrysome Lad
I've a hunger for rings
round replete things
tarry not kumquat
kicks about low now—Quicken
Put up the banns!

Quicken to come Life open
up Bride ReceiveResieveReleave
ReliveReviveReveal HIS
ESSENCE Give life to Mouth
Music rose air surrender Your
slow ways Ole Norse *kvikna* Quick
Now lit wick lick *the reed* burns
as fast as he comes Ole English
gecwician Gee Wiccan not what
she once were powder keg her
wash the bride in whisky Put a spell
on coffin Our bearin bairn *Hit*
was whirmed awa Quick bring
One back return from Urn
Yearner departed delights
'taking real pleasure in a
broken night' falling and
waking up Again and
again REGENERATE
'to hasten accelerate
impart speed to' Pick
up Yer pace IN Her
riding for Yer life now
Gie it laldy with gusto
'become faster more
active' in the climb Of
a woman 'enter the
state of' EMBOLI 'in
which the chile gives
indications of life'
Stroke her building
blocks brew
th'eighteenth week
keep away common
rue Guard hard the
lightning gentle streak a
slight shift in belly hue

Ah *approach the altar*

with forked tongue

with lightning tongue

Sudden blinding

buzzing tongue

Pollinate her

Chanting I do

I do I do

I do what

Wed

Épouser

Take in

Betrothed

Ballad maker

Blindfolded

labia

Insurmountable

meaning

You couldn't climb

on top of Me with

britches on

'Spondere'

Make offering

Spontaneous airy bare

Perform a rite

Promise secret

Engage oneself

by ritual act

Secrete the secret

Light fir candles light reeds for Our passage

to be read by

fur bare flight Buddleia field

fluttering rinds ring purpureal scent

pin It down unlock last quiver pearly crescent

If marriage is a sentence

How long will We

Leave out the full

Stop Your hands tremble
Loch Leven Fife flax
Weary weave
that clunking sound
every time you warp and weft
Whole earth heaves with
Ephemeral lines linen
Bundled Bairns
Born and gone Beyond
All from saying
Two lightning struck
words
I do I do
I do lasts and I do not
last I am
impermanent

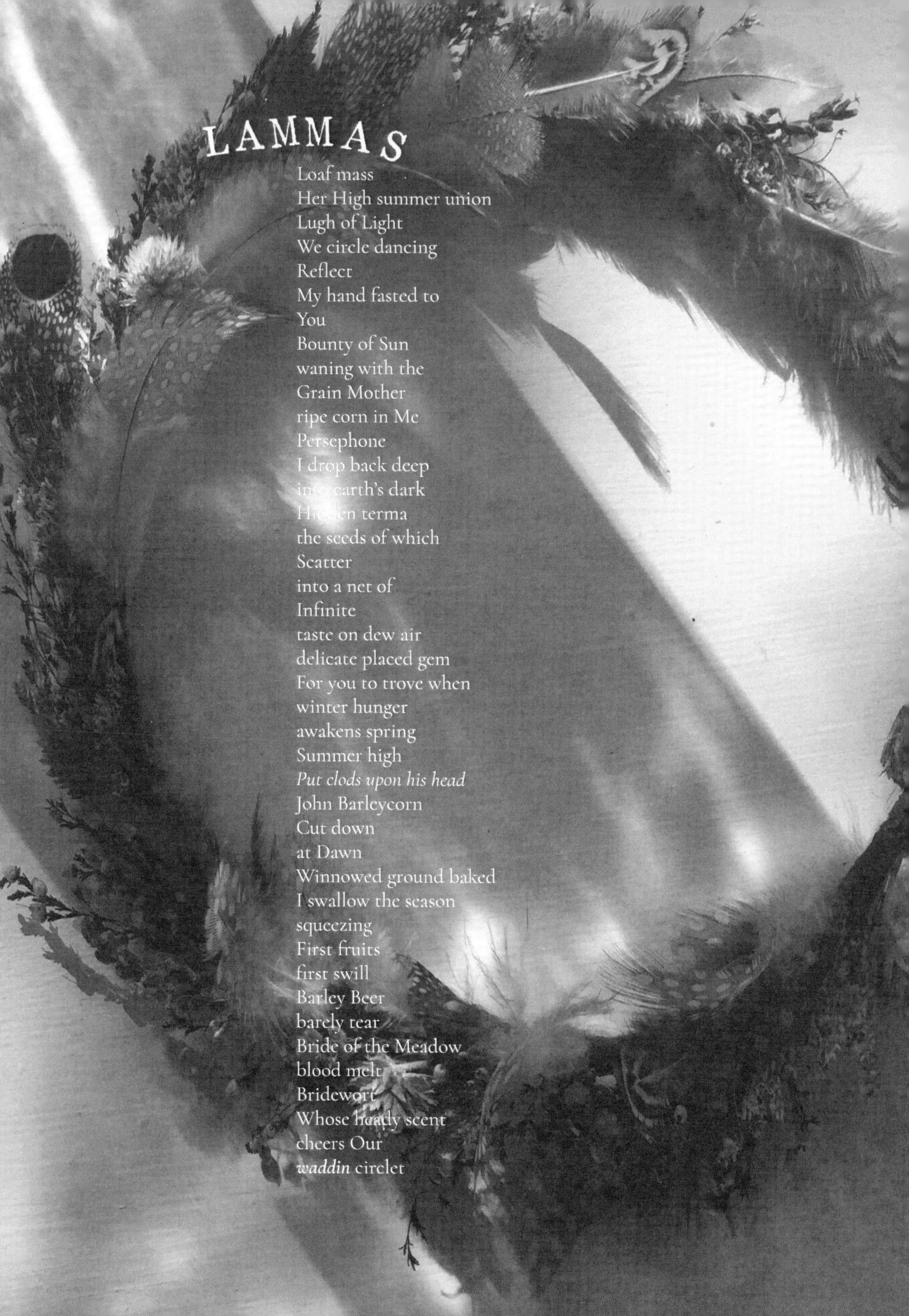

LAMMAS

Loaf mass
Her High summer union
Lugh of Light
We circle dancing
Reflect
My hand fasted to
You
Bounty of Sun
waning with the
Grain Mother
ripe corn in Me
Persephone
I drop back deep
into earth's dark
Hidden terma
the seeds of which
Scatter
into a net of
Infinite
taste on dew air
delicate placed gem
For you to trove when
winter hunger
awakens spring
Summer high
Put clods upon his head
John Barleycorn
Cut down
at Dawn
Winnowed ground baked
I swallow the season
squeezing
First fruits
first swill
Barley Beer
barely tear
Bride of the Meadow
blood melt
Bridewort
Whose heady scent
cheers Our
waddin circlet

Not much planning
needed
a quick
meal Together
Homebound
gathering close
post nuptials
muslin draped
slung across the back of
My hand tied
bouquet
purples
heather bound
muirs

Friends
undress us
complete
ceremony
in Our
bed chamber
My stockings
O'er shoulder
Fly away
wilted petals
to One Who
will soon wed
Spirits willing
music drink chortles
Night chews through
They won't
Leave Us till
We're full
Jug-bitten
too tap
hackled to
Needle thread
swoon back
lone bone
At Last!
bare bed

Be it warm and
            dry here heaven
wrapped in Us
            You glimmer cross-
ing those ten
            barley shook miles
Your compass
            barely took pantiles
My candle
            lit for You
climbing up My
            and You so cold
from outer wet
            'Here come in'
to My Warm
            reign this little
bodie hearth
            cresting with
zeal and sewn
            bare to You

First ubiquitous pine, as in 'pine for love,'
a romantic fugue is never over.
~ Anne Waldman

Bundling
interludes &
italic-chords within
woven from
lunga-held notes
below:

A Helen Adam Reader, Helen Adam & Kristin Prevallet

Principles of Midwifery; or, Puerperal Medicine, John Aitken, M.D.

The Veiled Suite: The Collected Poems, Agha Shahid Ali

A Glossary of the Shetland Dialect, James Stout Angus

Auden, W.H. Auden

Pride and Prejudice, Jane Austen, adapted by Andrew Davies

Sense and Sensibility, Jane Austen, as retold by Ang Lee & Emma Thompson

Petticoats and Prejudice: Women and Law in Nineteenth-Century Canada, Candace Backhouse

"A Time and Place for Premarital Desire: Positive Uses of Lust in Edmund Spenser's *The Faerie Queene,*" Rachel Balzar

Sappho, Mary Barnard Trans.

Bringing Back the Fire, Kimberly Becker

Auguries of Innocence & Songs of Experience, William Blake

Outside History, Eavan Boland

Dictionary of Phrase and Fable, E. Cobham Brewer

Aurora Leigh, Elizabeth Barrett Browning

Pippa Passes, Robert Browning

"Bide a start wi me," Rhoda Butler

"So, we'll go no more a roving," Lord Byron

"'He came to her bed pretending courtship': sex, courtship and the making of marriage in Ulster, 1750-1844," Leanne Calvert

"Evadné," René Char

Fugitive Suns, Andrée Chedid; Lynne Goodhart & Jon Wagner, trans.

"Meadow Season" Andrée Chedid; Marci Vogel, trans.

ABCs, Neeli Cherkovsky

Lady of the Lotus-Born, Gyalwa Changchub and Namkhai Nyingpo

The Third Body/ Le troisième corps, Hélène Cixous

Stigmata: Escaping Texts, Hélène Cixous

"New Amsterdam," Elvis Costello

"J'ai tant rêvé de toi," Robert Desnos

A Circle of Songs, Ed Dorn

The Art of Bundling, Dana Doten

Wishing Well, "Laddie, Lie Near Me," Connie Dover

The Collected Early Poems and Plays, Robert Duncan

At Day's Close: Night in Times Past, A. Roger Ekirch

Art & Love: An Illustrated Anthology of Love Poetry: Kate Farrell, ed.

"Ribinnean Rìomhach," Puirt-A-Beul, Julie Fowlis

Sheela-Na-Gig, Unravelling an enigma, Barbara Freitag

Secret of the Ron Mor Skerry, Rosalie K. Fry

"Je t'aime, . . . Moi non plus," Serge Gainsbourg, as performed Gainsbourg, & Cat Power

The Mistress Bradstreet, Charlotte Gordon

Romantic Outlaws: The Extraordinary Lives of Mary Wollstonecraft & Mary Shelley, Charlotte Gordon

Art poétique, Eugène Guillevic

No Death, No Fear, Thich Nhat Hanh

Teachings on Love, Thich Nhat Hanh

The Woodlanders, Thomas Hardy

Online Etymology Dictionary, Douglas R. Harper

Priest/ess 28: Pubic Ubiquity, j/j hastain

The Malachim Conglomerate, j/j hastain

Day Has No Equal But Night, Anne Hebert

"Inversnaid," Gerard Manley Hopkins

"The Wedding in Scots," Dr. Dauvit Horsbroch

The Nonconformist's Memorial, Susan Howe

Ce sexe qui n'en est pas un/This Sex Which Is Not One, Luce Irigaray

"Our story of Dhaka Muslin," *AramcoWorld,* Khademul Islam

Finnegan's Wake, James Joyce

"Ode to a Nightingale,"; "La Belle Dame sans Merci," John Keats

The Secret Commonwealth of Elves, Fauns, & Fairies, Rev. Robert Kirk

A Curious History of Sex, Kate Lister

Martha Lloyd's Household Book, "Martha's Receipt for Ink," Martha Lloyd

The Kalevala, an epic poem after oral tradition, Elias Lonnrot, Keith Bosley, trans.

A Drunk Man Looks at the Thistle, Hugh MacDiarmid

"Lover Come Back to Me," Jeanette MacDonald and Nelson Eddy

"Eve of Easter," Bernadette Mayer

"Distinctive semantic fields in the Orkney and Shetland dialects, and their use in local literature," J. Derrick McClure

Gràs, "Leanabachd," Mairi McInnes

Moby-Dick, Herman Melville

Lieder ohne Worte, Songs Without Words, Felix Mendelssohn

Songs of Milarepa, Milarepa, John Murray, trans.

"We Can Live on Love," Glen Miller Orchestra

Bringing Down the Colonel, Patricia Miller

"Great Clouds of Blessings: The Prayer That Brings All Existence Under One's Command," Jamgön Mipham Rinpoche

Sleeping with the Dictionary, Harryette Mullen

The View from Castle Rock, Alice Munro

Collected Works, Lorine Niedecker

"Distress and Benevolence on Gertrude Fitzgerald's Limerick Estate in the 1840s," Desmond Norton

Cantos, Ezra Pound

"Promises like Pie-Crust," Christina Rossetti, as sung by Carla Bruni

Henry VI, Shakespeare

The Tempest, Shakespeare

"The Masque of Anarchy, Written on the Occasion of the Massacre at Manchester," Percy Bysshe Shelley

Dakini's Warm Breath, Judith Simmer-Brown

Bundling: A Curious Courtship Custom, Elmer Smith

Elles: A Bilingual Anthology of Modern French Poetry by Women, Martin Sorrell, trans.

Bundling: Its Origin, Progress and Decline in America, Henry Reed Stiles

Tender Buttons, Gertrude Stein

"Yes, They Did Wear Them: Working Class Women and Corsetry in the 19th Century," Leigh Summers

A Thoughtful Soul: Reflections from Swedenborg, Emmanuel Swedenborg, George Dole, trans.

"I am too close for him to dream of me," Wisława Szymborska

Gitanjali, Rabindranath Tagore

Larkrise to Candleford, Flora Thompson

A Scots Dictionary of Nature, Amanda Thomson

La Scienza Nuova, Giambattista Vico

"Future Burnt of Leaves," Anne Waldman (read in memorium of Bernadette Mayer at Woodberry Poetry Room, December 8, 2022)

Marriage: A Sentence, Anne Waldman

Vow to Poetry, Anne Waldman

"Brooklynease," Lewis Warsh (read by Bernadette Mayer at his memorial, April 24, 2022)

"The Corset," Lewis Warsh

Lyrical Ballads, William Wordsworth & Samuel Taylor Coleridge

If Walls Could Talk: An Intimate History of the Home, Lucy Worsley

Fairy & Folk Tales of Ireland, W. B. Yeats

Further Notes:

Front Cover Image: Louie Fuller dancing.
Back Cover Image: Louie Fuller dancing, by Samuel Joshua Beckett,
décollaged with "The snowdrop, 1807," by Robert John Thornton.
Cover Designs: T Thilleman & Author.
Lithograph, page 33: Pierre-Philippe Choffard, *Marchez tout doux, parlez tout bas,* 1782.
Quilt on page 34 handstitched by Jane Austen and her sisters.
Recipe for ink, on page 330, by Martha Lloyd, Austen's friend.
"Old Coins Placed in the Wish Tree on Isle Maree," photograph, page 301.
Aerial Photograph of Inchmahome Priory, Scotland, 2016, page 341.
Colophon: "Only the visions of this state...," Robert Duncan, Preface to *Caesar's Gate.*

Gratitude to the unknown soul who created the visual collages—which make up the background images in *Bundling*—found on an antique screen recently uncovered in a New England attic. Photos of these collages are by Author.

Proposal poem, page 203, from Author's third great grandfather, Michael Callaghan, to Author's third great grandmother, Johanna McCarthy, an Irish orphan girl, in Melbourne, Australia, 1860.

Photograph, page 305, of 1865 King James Bible with Blake clipping, from Author's grandmother, Adele, via Author's mother. Bible was passed from Abbott Brown (Author's 3rd great grandfather) to his daughter, Adelia (Author's 2nd great grandmother), in 1867, then gifted to Adele on the eve of her wedding, 1922.

Many of the backstories in *Bundling* are true accounts of lived folk experiences recorded in various source documents. If curious about these backstories—or interested in studying the "strange" phrases herein—please peruse Fermata for further details.

Since in the palace of mind which transcends duality
I am waiting, waiting for the spiritual experience as my bride,
I have no time for setting up house.

~ Milarepa

Much Gratitude

Thank you to Truong Tran, whose inquiry inspired this project, and MFA classmates at San Francisco State who contributed insightful energy toward its first fruition. Thank you to Geoff Desa, for offering kind support in the early stages. Thank you to Marcia Woods, for initially informing me about the curious courtship custom. Thank you to Aurelia Lavallee, for transcendent editing and ethereal friendship. Mountainous thanks to j/j hastain, Priest/ess, for ever-musing on Beloved practice. To my Read-Her, the You who repletes Me, Sweet T. Marianne Vold, celestial celebrant. Kevin Quattrin, for generous genealogical research into the Callaghans, our ghost family. Thank you to Katie Parry, for illuminating the vitality of calligraphic threads; and to Anna Wu Weakland, for teaching me the Qi of each brushstroke. Megan O'Patry, kindred mouth musician. Lisa Panepinto, for providing lyrical light and spiritual succor. Richard Martin, steadfast poet, lightning-wise Mind. Richard Blevins, Duncan's bright star. Myah Garrison, the bard, for inspiring a future view. Dodo and Babu, for offering playful respite in all imaginable weather. George Dole, treasure-teacher, who illuminates Swedenborg, even now, among Angels. Anne Waldman, who embodies the Three Jewels: Wisdom, Compassion, and Beatific Vision. Eternal thanks and longevity to my Sangha, the Dharma bearers—Dharmata Foundation, Abhaya Fellowship and Sravasti Abbey—especially my teachers—who guide me on the Noble Path. All merit is shared; all mistakes are my own.

Heather Woods is the author of *Light Bearing* (Spuyten Duyvil 2015) and *Still Shall Hear a Calling Bell* (Spuyten Duyvil 2022). Her work was recently featured in the award-winning indie documentary: *Poetry, New York*, and the anthology: *Resist Much Obey Little: Inaugural Poems of the Resistance* (Dispatches Editions). By day, she teaches writing to students of all ages; by dawn, she selects and edits books for publication. She served as a member of Kelsey St Press in Berkeley and co-founded Persimmons literary magazine at Kenyon College. There she studied poetry, and in the San Francisco Bay Area, her native home. (Before her, four generations of her matrilineal ancestors and five of her patrilineal ancestors settled round The Golden Gate in The Golden State.) Seeking sustainable simplicity, Woods moved across the wide country to a wild woodland jutting off the Northern Atlantic Coast. Here she dwells with her beloved in a nearly two-hundred-year-old ship-mason's home. In this cold clime, in this storied house, there is no heat upstairs, and come winter, they verily practice The Bundling.

Only the visions of this state

this bardo

to sustain me.

That there was still vision was All.

These mere poems

contrived however they were

responded to the whispering angels

of the language.

It is because

in devotion to the art

or in self-indulgence

we shape ourselves

that this shaping

this making

by which we are

M A K A R I S

is divine.

Reading *Bundling*

Hi Heather,

Here some of my impressions after the initial reading of your work (jotted down as I read). I am mindful in a work of this magnitude; I most likely have missed much. I believe it took Joyce seventeen years to write *Finnegan's Wake* and that readers would be chasing down allusions for many many years. I can see from your extensive 'fermata' the fuel for your creative imagination.

Bundling is a magnificent epic (or is it a petite épopée or neither) and work of art. Its linguistic brilliance and formal beauty create a challenging polis for the mind to consider and inhabit. Without a doubt, a woman's form is supreme, and the voice(s) of the heroine ignites the "speech of many spirits /at once, / undulating like a scroll."

I will admit I never heard of "bundling" and my historical knowledge of Shetland, Scotland, England in particular during the late 18th century and 19th century is somewhat limited. Example, I didn't know about the Battle of Peterloo and found myself scrambling to read about it (a very positive side effect during the read). But I did have a decent view of the Irish landscape and Shetland. I could place my mind in Shetland as I read the poem. It's a place I want to visit. Thanks to a detective series situated there, I saw the gorgeous, tough landscape of the island and those who live there now. It was easy to assume bundling would be called for during the winter months. But I'm drifting here.

As I moved through the first 100 pages or so, I found the poetic excavation of the past of a premarital practice via modernist (innovative, original, challenging) and postmodern literary (time appropriation/history/anti-authoritarian, multiple style and poetic forms, dialects) sensibilities and techniques exposed every nerve of love and desire. The varied poetic forms— short line, imagistic, employing rhyme at times gained energy and power as the eye and mind moved down the lines. The heat of desire and love while wrapped in coverings, negotiating the sacred board. The poems employing projective verse offered the space to wander, rest, slow the pace of the read. Wrapped poems were a great innovation...full of information and insights...and challenging. The poems across the beautiful collages were a treat. Reflective...spacious, time to reconsider and move forward. The dialectic of love came into play at times. As Hélène Cixous writes: "real love....is a phantom touching"...."Eat me up, my love, or else I'm going to eat you up" ...with your lovely synthesis..."Hush Dear I hear the/ Mouth of swallows/ within You." Throughout the pages in poems and/or lines within, lyrics sing with power and beauty. They melted the mind and freed the spirit.

But bundling didn't always work or desire attain its goal. Nerves experience pain, disappointment and loss. When the woman loses her "bairn" and her lover is a drunk, the deepest and penetrating insights on the disappointments and anger attending love so often are given voice. The narrative of the epic had me now. I went batshit reading how the elders squeezed her teats to detect milk to confirm that sexual intercourse and a pregnancy had occurred.

Bundling embodies current threads: "*When/ does the Present/ become the Past*" (and vice versa, I believe). I happened to be reading the bundled poem "Rue" at the time of the Supreme Court decision on Roe vs Wade. The Elders in Black Robes doing more or less the same thing in the present as in the past. In fact, the poem had the effect of surfacing the past into present...in particular for the oppressive history women have faced through the course of time. The freedom of love could also beckon tragedy and loss. As in the last lines of the poem (with threads of Anne Waldman): "Whole earth heaves with/ Ephemeral lines linen/ Bundled Bairns/ Born and Gone/ All from saying/ Two lightning struck/ words/ I do I do/ I do last and I do not/ last I am/ impermanent." All created beings vanish into Creation.

But onward. Eventually, the heroine seeks release to be an antinomian nomad via the grace of God and not a constructed moral code. But that's not all for she perceives the divine in nature, realizes the delusion of personal ownership...any ownership of people or the planet.

The heart-center of the book shakes with prayerful protests urging us to "Rise, like lions after slumber." Here the revolutionary echoes of Shelley resurface, and heartening Tagore sings out: "let my country awake." You use the bundling fabric to weave a wide expansive view of people and planet eternally harmed by colonial rule. Gave me a shiver, reading of the recent Capitol riots embedded here, tracing roots of white supremacy. When heroine proclaims, "Are you a proud/ Boy stand back." You remind us "There is no safe/ Harbor." The history of enslaved peoples is woven into the bundling sack and nightdress made of "clotted cotton/ in blood lit chains." And with your focus on continental bundling fabric, "Muslin," you spread the cloth wide to the British empirical dismemberment of Bengali artist-weavers: "Colonial/ Years tore/ Thumbs/ Weavers hands/ Mangled." *The Veiled Suites* of Agha Shahid Ali...who used imagination to weave past and present imperialisms...quiver here with fresh urgency. Bundling backstories are clearly carefully researched and honor the people past, bringing them fully present. Not without some sardonic examination of our virtual virtue-signaling culture: "How brightly we/ fancy Ourselves/ Abolitionists/ Fancy Ourselves/ Full stop." This chapter culminates with the displacement/destruction of Native peoples and land. Collective colonial karma coming to haunting fruition: "No shelter from/ What's to come." In the horrifying final poem, "Inversnaid," the rabid hunter is shooting everything that moves and mothers until there is nothing left to hunt.

Again, the fucked-up present...living on a planet the Homo sapiens species is hellbent to destroy the Garden (planet Earth)... species and plant extinction on land and sea compliments of us....

and again the Supreme Court...limits EPA the authority to curb carbon emissions from power plants. Choke. Choke. Your epic brings to life through imagery and detail the Garden about to be destroyed as the century turns into the Industrial Revolution...life abounds through the pages of the work. The heroine sees it all... and instructs the mind to remember the opening line: *Because the expanse of reality is not I.* "I" is a construct like every other construct the mind overlays on the expanse of reality only to be befuddled by the illusions and delusions it creates and is responsible for and in denial of.

When are we going to wake up?

And back to the imagery..."nights like this/ frost lipped kiss/ tree limb tinged"....such a tight and perfect image....all through the epic and all the Gaelic, Scottish, Old English words and rhythms... some defined in the course of the poem, the takeoff from that... always surprising.

The magnetism of sensuality and spirituality pulses through the work (romantic, erotic, transcendent)..."I want to be tied up 'bundlin' with You till death us Do." The work "bundled" my attention. I felt at times I was on a literary space voyage into the past, a retrieval of the spacetime actually there, a living presence the past. I was lost at times but excited about being lost....the opportunity to discover.

As I proceeded more and more into the book, I began to feel more and more bundled, drawn into the interior landscape and vortex of a woman in a particular time period (but relevant to anytime period, including the present)— her consciousness and perceptions, acute, critical, political, spiritual, beautiful. Transcendence. Expanded Consciousness...the birth of Being. The physical and metaphysical purposes and implications of Sheela na gig and Mother Doula. Fecundity of the very dirt in the veins...where you come from where you go...the w(HOLE) So seeing the divine in nature...but the flesh and bones of that...i.e...the actual ground...the fertile ground...the sacrifice of first lamb to the goddess for a good harvest to survive...to understand and revere Mother Earth...the body of her...in ecstatic harmony with the sun. . .with light...Being there...but not only are we destroying the flesh and bones of the literal earth (throughout the poem dug literary archeology. . .) we move further away from it...into virtual space...eyes locked on screens of fantasy...blindness to the sacred beauty from which we and everything arises...the interconnectedness of all things... wake up clergy...Supreme Court. Mostly men and clergy to a great extent thinking they can legislate a woman's body...encased it in a moral code. Drunk husbands, Elders, Pillocks, class distinctions via women high to whore...oppressive sexual mores of the time/of our time.

For me, the heroine of the epic offers an odyssey of love, loss repercussions, banishment...and the struggle and intelligence to free herself from it all...the microscopic-cultural chains, doctrines and opinions until her voice, and/or the voice(s) of the poem and/or spirits undulating down a scroll into the Expansion of Consciousness. The earth in its glory and divinity. It's wild proliferation of life...not the extinction of it by greedy little minds soaked in the poison of ownership and power. *Bundling* ignites the mind for growth and understanding. And then the woman (for me) morphed into the Muse of the Woods, the ascendent woman on the cover with a crown of clouds and orange ball of moon.... her vaporous garments encompassing all...softly transcendent and there as if the Blessed Virgins statues in my neighborhood became animated and rose into the atmosphere. On a flight via the wood of words via a planchette with a pencil dancing on automatic writing. *Listen the trees are shedding words, the mind storming with birds.* Write. But then I dozed off...old man asleep in the middle of the afternoon...then to my desk with the automatic pen of dictation (to write):

Awake

Outside a misplaced window
a fire burns
I roll my days in a page of clouds
thread through a raindrop
as a flower opens
with dusted wings
I've been distracted before
lost in the woods
of the soul
as you danced across
the branches of the world
I caught your scent in the redolent
ambience of memory
Maybe
I must return to the present
awake in a sky of blue water
Contagion of time bewitches
You understand this
conversing with wind
I stand wherever I am
searching for a window
of clues
in ethereal smoke

But then as I turned to final part of the book...I was back to every nerve of love and desire exposed/revealed, a transcendent coupling of sensuality and spirituality as in the lines "ravish Me/ make My invisible/ visible divine." Physical, sexual love manifests divine love....union with divinity (God/Creator) i.e. "You will find me dwelling in the heart of every being." The flash of oneness in blood and bones. Or as the lines suggest...lyrics from the unconscious and "Make yer own meaning." We are transcendent beings made of Stardust. One with the One whether we know it or not. So, the poem propels the mind into expanded/cosmic consciousness via its finite bones. The wonderful complexity and simplicity in the mirror of a shattered dialectic.

Or *Bundling* blasts the body-soul-mind as one into Creation... as I sit on my back porch with a cup of coffee, the morning sun illuminating my mind, warming my skin with its goodness. My golden retriever feels it, luxuriates in the morning as I pet her. Stillness in the city (ok some noise) but the neighborhood birds in their morning conversations mute it. The bed of tiger lilies turned in unison to the light with the glee they feel...trumpeting the universal truth of the moment. So, a sip of coffee as a beautiful emptiness cascades in my blood…soaking in oneness as inside & outside vanish in their shadows and cloud cover. *Bundling* the match...igniting "spasms of joy" across the pages.

There is no way for me to claim I grasped the work in its all its grandeur. It's too complex on a first read over a few weeks (I could be completely off in everything I've written). Fly off the language on the page into my own initial gestalt (as to the nerves, a realization and celebration of ecstasy...opening the pores of self/ being to Being through acts of love and vision though tempered and transformed along the way by the lonely holes of loss in the heart into wisdom). It's a poem to be studied. To communicate with someone about...to share information…Like hey, walking around Shetland with you. I got slowed down via the dialect at times and my own lack of Celtic Scottish Welsh and English lore. I knew about about fairies and elves and druids (think some of them lived in my house as kid)...but I never heard of Cerridwen goddess of the cauldron...and enchantress, Celtic Goddess of Inspiration, but was happy to meet her and thought you might be in direct communication with her. The work inspires inspiration. And more.

The bundled poems, as mentioned, offered critical information and insights...and valuable entomological information...

FECUNDITY for example. Liked it all...waves of immediate accessibility...waves of studied accessibility. I thought at times a glossary of at least some of the terms not immediately revealed in the next line might have helped me. I remember looking up *alfadl, alfsogoda, ylfe* to understand malevolent elves and the diseases they cause. But I loved how spirits and lore percolated across the poem and informed it...The woman certainly was able to perceive spirits...and beyond them recognize the divine in nature as I mentioned. There were many individual poems I loved throughout the collection...for ex....the one on page 283...that starts with: "To be with leaves/ as they spring off the branch/ one last dance"...and ends..."pearl mist owre/ a kiss from spirits/ afore"—nature spirits and dialect in harmony, shaped by beauty of content and form.

Autumn

It's been too noisy in my brain. I
need the comfort of leaves, falling
from trees.

I should abandon my chair, enter
the wind as a leaf.

Congratulations!

Dick

Richard Martin
Author of *Chapter & Verse*
July 7, 2022
West Roxbury, Boston

Opening *Bundling* feels like opening a cedar chest full of not only herstorical truths, and residue from elements once lived, but full also of the internal her-stories as yet untold. Woods uses collages, images, calligraphy, found texts and timely documents to bring the pass-ed voices into the living now. Violations and violences upon Her body are fully present, as well as the blood and gore of inhabiting female form: "with heath/ aether rich soil/a smoldering scent/ Her body/ cinders."

Or opening *Bundling* is like holding a glowing faerie book, where sinful sirens' sound emits. Seductively sonorous herstorical her stoical lyric documentary where history is a weave gathering in the Three Times. Bundling is, in practice and art form, Syncretistic, drawing together elements from many traditions. *Bundling* expands its legs wide across continents, mother-languages and narratives to take in large hard truths. The poems contract and expand in bundles and release in sacred flight Earth and peoples severed by colonial patriarchy's narrow lexicon. "Sowans/ sewin her own/ language to/ speak to the spirits/ In." Grabbing the phallus to write her view. "History is written/ by those who hold/ the Quill." Here a synesthesia of spirit: ritual traditions correspond with newborn fruitions. She shakes up the glazed empirical colonial gaze: "there is no holy state/ as long as He profits/ all is taint." She asks us to question precedent and embark upon that climb toward the Third Eye view: "How is this life/ interacting with/ the Others."

A mistress of form, Woods wends the deconstructed sonnet and smashed ballad alongside the ghazal and explodes all with sapphic fragments that haunt and moan. Both a Poet's poet and a folk poet, Woods embodies the human plight's flight. A masterful work of many lifetimes, her wide weave takes up history and shakes it askew to examine our current quandaries. Intricately collaging sound, text and image, she renews history through fierce empathy. Casts a spell. The burdens and joys of the flesh. The spiritual is from the earth, "Mother May I hear/ The Green Goddess near/ Turn the wheel of the Tongue/ flicking clouds." Against material duality, here poverty becomes a maternal richness. "'The nearer the bone/ the sweeter/ the meat.'"

Bundling, like the female orgasm, goes on forever, pleasureful. Revivifying endless epiphanies, tingly. She shoots her wad into the stars. Cum-passion. Profoundly researched from source texts and listening with attuned empathy to myriad voices, "a kiss/ from spirits/ afore." Intimacy counter to technocracy. Eros triumphs here. Despite innumerable obstacles, Love prevails. She straddles the fluid duality of male and female then weaves a wondrous Between: "Any body/ Could be/ Mother." An epic épopée from a fluid and expansive mind. Yab-yum. You bundled to me. Oh holy now. I am in Love.

~ j/j hastain, Author of *Priestless*

***Bundling* is a vibrant powerhouse**, at once fresh and ancient, sensuous and reverent. Heather Woods bears witness to society's inhumanities while defending the sanctity of all beings in this collection. These poems move deftly between traditional forms such as couplet, illumination, persona, opus, and historical narrative into experimental hybrid, protest, and prayers for protection of the oppressed. Sonic rhapsodies, ingenious wordplay, and tantric unions provide divine sustenance as euphoric scenery and radiant tenderness shelter us through the night. This book is an exquisite treasure.

~ Lisa Panepinto, Author of *Where I Come From the Fish Have Souls*

Heather Woods's *Bundling* understands how intimate strands of language hold us in anticipation for pleasure. Each poem is tightly wound to feel each intricate fiber, each delectable pulse. Here content is woven with form to conjure the tradition of bundling. As she quotes Hélène Cixous, "Real love is a / don't touch, yet still an / almost-touching. / A phantom touching," the real longing occurs within the lingering haunts of sensuality. As readers we are also just beyond grasp of physicality that leaves us enchanted by her text.

~ C. M. Chady, Author of *Embodied Unconscious: the feminine space of sexuality, surrealism, and experimentation in literature*

***Bundling* by Heather Woods is a master work**, a tome of more than four hundred pages of sensually charged poetry exploring Bundling : to sleep in the same bed fully clothed, a custom formerly practiced in New England and the British Isles. With her wonderful sense of the music inherent in language, Heather Woods bundles a very progressive use of language, while never losing sight of the necessity of the poetry to be of use to the human condition. I remembered while reading that William Carlos Williams said: all art is sensual, Heather Woods's poetry is successful, marvelous. It is poetry that remains consistently erotic and consistently poetically innovative and progressive. This is a magical event for poetry. Her poetry bundles need and want.

~ Michael Basinski, Author of *Tub Bunny*

Heather Woods's *Bundling*—located in a Pagan/Christian eighteenth-century Kingdom of Great Britain and Ireland, faintly colored by pigments of Tibetan Buddhism—is a sensory investigation of coupling. In a plurality of voices and as visual spectacle, these experiential poems sing of the fluidity that combines personal and cultural customs, beginning with "bundling," a courting tradition in which couples are wrapped and bound to sexually enrapture one another. From bundling to delivering a bundle of joy, **Bundling basks in the slippery, the smear,** the waxy, the excrement, the slathering of the bawdy spirit of the body for the most human of pleasures. Many of the peak moments conveyed are prayers of lovers' mystery, uttered under the dim glow of moonlight. Languages bound and bundled to time and place disrobe and marry in these poems, unveiling deep roots of intimacy and humor.

~ Martine Bellen, Author of *Ghosts!*

bundling **is a splendid grace of generosity.** it opens itself to a myriad of other texts of desire, of our human urgency for physical intimacy at the heart of spiritual and emotional connection. the food of life. and it is generous in being a kind of medieval illuminated book, whose design simply delights. heather woods's original writing, her poems herein, variously lyrically coy, subtly nimble, openly inviting—inspire all of this in all of us.

~ Martin Nakell, Author of *consciousness*

Heather Woods unveils the polite yet brutal custom of "bundling," surreptitiously revealing lust and its lush curtain of seduction, as it becomes clear that bundling, cruel as it may have been, represents the art of foreplay, which goes on subtly and secretly, initiating true caution, true fear, true as guardians of the heart/mind/body on the ornate precipice of desire—that ornateness represented in the elaborate design of this remarkable book, an extravagantly illustrated volume. Weaving together (beyond mere bundling) external texts with her own poetry, Woods writes demurely sensuous poems which can't help but entice us into a very satiating reading experience.

~ Rebecca Goodman, Author of *Forgotten Night*

"Poems by the Bundles: Heather Woods's *Bundling*"

the Two of us / mingled Side / by mingled Bound

Bundling is what we have from a poet's trance of overhearing, a record of bundlers' night-long talks. Heather Woods's intimate poem of many pages is throughout so thoroughly human that it seems the very future of feminism. Historical bundling kept courting couples warm in a chaste bed; but the church-sanctioned practice also enabled the creation of private worlds of lovers' pillow talk in an otherwise workaday existence. In Woods's treatment, the dualities of bundling become a grand subject. Looking back to imagine, the bundling bag and board appear to be inventions of both pious practicality and erotic encasement. In his pamphlet from 1938, *Little Known Facts About Bundling in the New World*, A. Monroe Aurand, Jr., writes: "Comfortably snuggled down into one of the enormous feather beds of the period, the lovers were at last in a position, literally and figuratively, to carry on uninterruptedly those fascinating, endless, intimate conversations which have been a prerequisite of enamored youth from the beginning of time." As he began, Aurand's historical society must have prayed for a scandal. But Woods has not written a book of titillating curiosities, and she assiduously eschews bundling as Americana (or what Dana Doten, one of her sources, has called "the curly maple of our American character"!). Woods imagines instead a rich folk anthropology, the poems arriving in bundles upon her "sewin her own // language to // speak to the spirits." Spirit practitioners of bundling come up and witness, more like Homer than Yeats, in the voices of farming and husbandry, male and female, Ruth but also Boaz, to speak *through* the poet who does not speak *for* them, much as it is for Odysseus in Book 11. Swedenborg, a key source for the poem, believed that gender survives death (*Conjugal Love*). Notably, Woods's rendering in open form of what turns out to be the big bag of bundling, and using the bundling board to write upon, unzips the once dichotomy and insists that Mind must form its freedom. One participant's ecstatic state outstrips the boundaries of even Lorine Niedecker, whose page remained bound for life to her Objectivist lineage:

I'm gonna stretch

Me legs

high as

Sky

writing

No sensible words

Between My lips

Make Yer own meaning

A product of poetic bundling is meaning, and making your own meaning. It might be said that Niedecker's intellectual bundling produced "For Paul." Fucking interjects anon a third and begins to spill a story like the one about Niedecker living in New York when she self-aborted twin fetuses, a story with an ending, closed form. Her lover's violently binding her poem "There's a better shine" beside Pericles in his *A Test* anthology did not result in a marriage. As she comes to recognize in the poem "LZ," her mentor required from her a poetry of stops—the expansive poems came only in her last years, with the freedom of "Wintergreen Rider," the aforementioned "Paen to Place," the two Jefferson poems, and the ones on Darwin and William Morris. At length, she realized "a pencil / for a wing bone," an open poetry more flight and diving than atonal chamber music.

Woods-inspired is freed to write as if Niedecker had never met Zukofsky. (After all, Adelaide Crapsey didn't need Pound to intuit her own imagism in another room of the British Museum. "Crapsey, Imagist" would never do for the PR.) The Feminist repatriation of Lorine Niedecker was canon by 2002; now, 20 years later, theory will need to catch up with Woods's poem. Read aloud, pages in *Bundling*—262 to 263, do nicely—might be easily taken for what Niedecker told Cid Corman was "folk inspired" poetry—elsewhere in the same book, words and lines bob and float across the page a la Ted Berrigan.

Heather Woods's genius finds humor too, like Hope for America forgotten in the bottom of an old bundling bag. A lover has bound his girl in "frocked Me feet cord." A girl exclaims "I'll freeze knot this winter." Another admonishes her lover to "Pull the wool over my thighs / gentler..." "Tarry not" and "Tarrying" pun on a term for bundling. A cheeky lad informs us mock piously: "Parsimony" is "to be merry the / night through / without need / of candle tallow."

Bundling is Woods's metaphor for metaphor, or the way fictions work in what Gerald Murnane calls the Mind, by the art of binding what must remain separateness. For the fortunate ones, bundling can make a diagram of influence, a love line between writers that is more than a glossary of poetic affinities. Pound launched the ship of Modernism on gushes about customs of love and a trickle of redactions from Remy de Gourmont and Cavalcanti. I have come to bundle *Bundling* with Niedecker's late masterpieces, picturing their talk making little white clouds inside the cold darkness. To prepare for writing this essay, I have several times alternated re-readings from Woods's poem and Niedecker's poem. Then I came across Murnane's confession that he has fallen in love for life with female characters in his books; this bundling being, after all, a surfeit of love in the mind.

Richard Blevins
Author of *The Art of the Serial Poem*
August 20, 2022

Congratulations on this amazing tome,
so rich in thought, word, sound, dharma, serious wit.
O kindred Spirit!

'We have ignorantly slumbered and pray the fierce lions rise'—a glorious rousing incentive crouched within the ethos of the formidable Heather Woods. All praise.

~ Anne Waldman, author of *Sanctuary*